Always Something More To Do

EDNA IRENE
A STORY OF FAMILY & SELFLESSNESS

Written by
Dennis Denman

First published by Ultimate World Publishing 2022
Copyright © 2022 Dennis Denman

ISBN

Paperback: 978-1-922714-83-1
Ebook: 978-1-922714-84-8

Dennis Denman has asserted his rights under the Copyright, Designs and Patents Act 1988 to be identified as the author of this work. The information in this book is based on the author's experiences and opinions. The publisher specifically disclaims responsibility for any adverse consequences which may result from use of the information contained herein. Permission to use information has been sought by the author. Any breaches will be rectified in further editions of the book.

All rights reserved. No part of this publication may be reproduced, stored in or introduced into a retrieval system, or transmitted in any form, or by any means (electronic, mechanical, photocopying, recording or otherwise) without the prior written permission of the author. Any person who does any unauthorised act in relation to this publication may be liable to criminal prosecution and civil claims for damages. Enquiries should be made through the publisher.

Cover design: Ultimate World Publishing
Layout and typesetting: Ultimate World Publishing
Editor: Marinda Wilkinson
Shutterstock cover photo license:
Winai Tepsuttinun-Shutterstock.com
ESB Professional-Shutterstock.com
Box background vector created by nikapeshkov - www.freepik.com

Ultimate World Publishing
Diamond Creek,
Victoria Australia 3089
www.writeabook.com.au

Dedication

To her three great grandchildren, Judd, Mika and Xara, this is an attempt to share a life, long gone before your birth in different times and a different place. Her story, streets and places survive today with little change and you are welcome to add your footsteps to the path.

Love Papa

Contents

Dedication   iii

Chapter 1: Ballarat, Birth, Family   1

Chapter 2: School Days   31

Chapter 3: The Great Depression at the Door   53

Chapter 4: Family Life and Motherhood   77

Chapter 5: A New Start in Melbourne   91

Chapter 6: A Home of Her Own   105

Chapter 7: Ups and Downs and Roundabouts   117

Chapter 8: Journey's End   149

About the Author   159

Contents

Ballarat Courier
Monday 5 August 1907
Cost: 1 penny

Births & Marriage

James: Mary Elizabeth and George Edwin
welcome their new daughter, Edna Irene
to their home in East Ballarat.
A beautiful, brown-eyed girl who joins her brother
George in our family.

Then followed:

Norman Wellesly, born 1911

John Leslie, born 1915

CHAPTER 1

Ballarat, Birth, Family

The city of Edna's birth was well established when she entered the world.

Much had changed and would change again and again in the period of her life.

Long gone the city of tents and the murmurings of a multitude of races. Long gone the rumble of cradles as the miners sought colour from washing the soil. Long gone the applause for Lola Montez entertaining the rich and hopefuls. Gone, the sounds of cheering as the Prince of York, along with his entourage and lackeys anointed the city with a royal visit.

Much had occurred in the place of her birth as the city and country entered the twentieth century. Although still administrated by two separate Councils, the dual cities of East and West were well on their way to consolidation.

The early Ballarat goldfields consisted of three distinct areas known as Ballarat East, Ballarat West and Nerrina. Gold taken from its natural gullies and creeks had fed the inflow of a population from every corner of the world. The weathered and dirty white of canvas tent cities had long been struck as the population consolidated or moved away. Some stayed beyond the rush, many moved as other locations boomed gold. Edna's grandparents had been part of that voracious immigration thirsty for riches and a better way of life.

Before her time, the waters of the Yarrowee Creek dividing the town from East and West was curtailed and spanned. Ballarat East's roads and byways had followed the contours of the landscape with rolling features as its street lines swept towards the west, with Victoria Street the main arrival destination from Melbourne. After much deliberation by the city councillors, the waters and run-off of the creek were completely covered over so they flowed under the CBD. Here the topography became a gentler plateau and the benefits of the State surveyor, W.S. Urquhart's, original block grid pattern unfolded. Sturt Street was laid out as a major promenade with a central reserve of trees and statues dividing traffic either side.

It was the city and its byways that the James family knew as home. While the family's immediate zone was Ballarat East and its institutions and lifestyle, Edna, along with her brothers, came to know all the streets in the surrounding areas. Stawell Street to Victoria Street and on to central Ballarat, all would be held in their memories.

The Golden City

Ballarat, the city that was to be her home for nearly 50 years, had its starting place as a rural pastoralist location some 70 miles (100 km) from Melbourne Port. Later, when Edna moved to Melbourne her hard work and independent spirit enabled a new life.

Back in the 1850s, half a century before Edna was born, Ballarat was awash with people that arrived from every corner of the world at the cry of 'Gold!'. Along with its rival city of Bendigo, Ballarat became the hub of Victoria, as immense wealth was taken from across and beneath its gullies and landscape. It had been the major gold centre of the then Colony of Victoria that hurtled the colony and city to fame in that earlier period. By 1854, Ballarat records a population increase of 40,000.

During that period, the city fathers had established a degree of infrastructure the envy of major cities. By the 1860s the local reservoirs were completed providing clean drinking water and Yuille's Swamp revamped into a recreational lake and wetlands now called Lake Wendouree. The Ballarat Zoological Gardens followed in the mid-1870s. More was to come.

In the preceding century, Australia was still seen by the majority of the population as English and by outsiders as an in-transient child of the British Empire with little impact on world affairs. The long reign of Queen Victoria ended with her passing, sending England and the dominions into a deep period of mourning. Yet the voice of the country was beginning to stir. Australia, even with Federation, retained its allegiance to the Crown and the 'White Australia policy' stood at the masthead. If you listened, varieties of the mother tongue could be heard merged with all manner of the languages of Europe and the ever-present Chinese minority.

The City of Ballarat falls within the traditional boundaries of the Kulin nation and custodians. However, it seems that the traditional owners of the land were never recognised in the past and little is mentioned of their presence or role as part of the Golden City.

At the time of Edna's birth, a new century was already challenging change of a different sort as Australia experienced Federation. The First Federal Government/Parliament had been established in Victoria's capital Melbourne, at the end of Port Phillip Bay on the banks of the Yarra River. As

Federation approached, a *Melbourne Age* columnist wrote, 'the old century went out amidst rain and storm: disunity and parochialism made a tearful exit'.

The scene was set for a new generation of Australians.

Coming of age

Welcome to the world

Edna Irene was born on a Sunday 4 August 1907 in the town of Ballarat East. The following day the local *Ballarat Courier* noted, '*Nothing of world significance was reported today*'.

Always Something More To Do

Not true – in their simple home in the town of Ballarat East, George and Mary James welcomed the birth of a daughter.

In Melbourne the day prior, the *Saturday Age* newspaper continued the style of the day with page after page of sales and advertisements, before reporting on local and world affairs. On the Monday following, the *Courier* noted the shipping report and arrivals at Melbourne. Steam ships from New Zealand, Sydney, Devonport and Fremantle. Coach timetables between Ballarat and Creswick with Cobb & Co leaving from Craig's Hotel.

Well old girl it's time to put some words to your tale. Words of greater substance than those pithy thoughts on the remembrance plaque set facing the morning sun at the Boroondara Cemetery, formally Kew Cemetery – Journey's End.

Whatever the final words or mark of memory, they seldom, I suspect, tell of the depth of loss of family and friends to become little more than a marker of life.

The final years leading to Journey's End can be somewhat unrelenting for those who reach their ninth decade. Those later years had seen Edna dislocated from her little home in Brougham Street, Kew and a series of health issues to which she fought with uncompromising courage. This old girl was a fighter and it was a characteristic of her life that she by circumstances and birth was destined to battle and

Ballarat, Birth, Family

place others long before her own needs and wants. In other times and cultures, if a totem was to represent her life it would be a symbol of selflessness.

The birth of a child is a special moment in all lives and as a shared experience her parents and grandparents would have been equally overjoyed. Edna Irene James was the second child and was to be the only female to survive of this young family. Earlier in this new twentieth century the James family had celebrated the arrival of their first born, her brother George Fredrick, Edna's eldest sibling. In later years two younger brothers, Norman Wellesley and John Leslie were additions to the family.

During this period her parents also lost two baby girls who failed to live beyond birth or early childhood adding two separate dark periods in the family's life.

Family was a conspicuous part of Edna's long life and whether from self-sacrifice or circumstances, she became a central part of succeeding families. Firstly her parents and later in her own, as her marriage to an eligible widower bought a ready-made family of three small boys.

Surely the times and period were against the women of her day but circumstances can lead to difficult life decisions. Women's right to vote in Victoria was achieved a year after her birth but had been enacted for the Commonwealth in 1902. Edna was to marry late in life having seen each of her brothers leave one after another. Each married local girls but only George Fredrick and his wife continued their lives in Ballarat. In 1935, George married Tous (formally named Elsie Mabel Parkes) and moved closer to the commercial centre, buying a residence in Magpie Street. Both John and Norman were to follow life's pattern and some years later flew the nest; John to marry Grace (Ethel Grace) Montgomery and together they moved to Melbourne. Almost a year to the day after his brother's nuptials, Norman married Gwen (Edith Gwendolin) Fraser at the St Peter's Church in Sturt Street, and soon after left for war service.

The Second World War had been raging in Europe since 1939 and from December of 1941 the Japanese war machine which had years before ruthlessly occupied Manchuria attacked the US navel forces in Hawaii. This was the commencement of the 'rising sun' turning south to occupy country after country in a merciless drive towards Australia.

Yet this was very much in the future and still unscripted.

Paternal family

Wind back the clock a century ago, and Edna and her brothers were second generation Australians. Like all immigrants, her forebears had travelled halfway across the world to settle in the Colony of Victoria to seek a better life. The time was the early 1850s when the announcement of gold in Australia rang around the world. Gold was first found in Clunes in June 1851.

Thousands had rushed to the diggings from distant lands as well as many employed at the docks and suburbs of Melbourne. History records that overnight men left their jobs, sailors jumped ship and in some suburbs of Melbourne not a man was left. Few found their fortunes, even though over 16 million ounces was taken from the district's alluvial deposits in those early years. Across the colony location after location trumpeted find after find, yet the regions of Ballarat and Bendigo were of greatest significance. Many left to follow other boom sites as the surface gold was cleaned away. Others stayed beyond this period to put down their roots and become part of a community. Edna's paternal and maternal grandparents were some of these.

On her paternal side, her grandfather John James's birthplace is noted as Cornwell, England. Her grandmother, Elizabeth Jane James was born in Plymouth, Devonshire, England. John is recorded as having arrived in the colony aboard the *Whirlwind* aged 22 in August 1862.

Elizabeth's family name was Brimblecombe and her marriage to John was to be the start point for successive generations on Australian shores. The Brimblecombes were reputed from family stories as having arrived in the colony in 1852, landing in either Williamstown or Portland and travelled overland to the site of the richest alluvial gold finds of the then Ballarat plains.

Keeping with the James line and those relatives who were linked to Edna and her then immediate family, Grandfather John James is a key player. George and Edna had been welcomed into a large wider family with an abundance of relatives as her father additionally had two older brothers, William Henry (1867) and John Alfred (1868), and a sister Florence Ethel (1884).

The celebration of the wider family is unknown but every family joins in welcome at the arrival of its newest member. Undoubtedly the good crockery and tea set would have pride of place with sponges and homemade cakes. Tea was the staple drink in every household as coffee had not yet become fashionable, if at all known. Tea it was for this family of faith as the demon drink had no place in this home. Regardless of the city's glut of hotels and grog shops this was not their way. Ballarat in the 1890s had an incredible 477 pubs declining to around 200 at the end of the boom. Tobacco was acceptable and her father's after dinner pipe remained a lifelong memory of Edna's.

Ballarat, Birth, Family

Our wonderful parents

On news of a safe arrival in the family, grandparents huff and puff a little and new uncles and aunts share the joy of the addition. Edna's family would have been no different at the time of her birth, with her paternal grandparents, Elizabeth Jane and John James near at hand.

Very much the family patriarch, JJ as he was referred to, had been successful in some earlier endeavours and now owned several rental properties in Stawell and Humffray streets and a flourishing general store at 283 Humffray Street North. Like many of his peers, he was an immigrant who had built his life far from his distant homeland.

John James's early occupation is recorded as a miner. At the time of Edna's birth the rate book notation is as a shopkeeper, so during his long life in his adopted country a degree of commercial and personal success had occurred. A simplistic interpretation may be that JJ's transition to a businessman may have been rapid and can surely only be associated with a successful find. From miner to shopkeeper and property owner was a micro story of a lucky few who found nuggets of gold from Clunes to Ballarat. In his will he is linked to the highly successful Temperance Mining Company and this together with his substantial property listing, became a backstory that saw Edna's father lose access and a share to a large financial windfall. JJ's last will and testament became the Gordian knot for which the family of George Edwin would never be able to untangle.

As was the generation of the time, JJ was a hard worker as were all who called themselves by occupation a miner. In that early period nearly all aspects of life revolved around an ability to compete with the elements and provide for a family. The first diggers had lived under canvas and rough timber shacks. Illustrated by many artists of the day, scenes depicted by the Austrian artist Eugene von Guerard and other notables like George Grant and Henry Winkle are today held in both private and national galleries.

Most of the earlier finds were taken from the ground or sluiced from the creeks and run-offs. As the years progressed shafts began to pock the landscape as the search took the committed miner deeper and deeper below ground. Years later as a man of means, JJ had some status in his community and is recorded as one of the founding trustees of the Humffray Street North church. The church records note it was built in 1866 by 'God faring Cornish miners who were not afraid of work'.

Established as a Bible Christian Church, it was one of four in Ballarat in 1870 – taking the name Methodist in 1901 after the Federation of Churches amalgamated. In the following years the impact on the James family and subsequent generations cannot be emphasised enough as this little church grew to provide community activities and functions. Beyond spiritual life there was the opportunity to participate in a wider social engagement, including the Tennis Club, Gymnasium, Cricket Club, Guilds and a Debating Society. The James family was part of a practising Christian faith.

Maternal family

Edna's father George Edwin married a Grant, Mary Elizabeth, who was one of three girls, along with Ethel Agnes and Jessie. They resided close by in Victoria Street, the main wide expansive roadway that became the east-west access to the communities of Ballarat. At the time of George Edwin and Mary Elizabeth's marriage, East Ballarat and West Ballarat were separate cities. Whether fact or fiction, records suggest that Edward Francis Grant had arrived about the same time as the James family arrived from Cornwell. Embarking from Plymouth, Edna's maternal grandfather Edward and family landed at Geelong and began their life in the outer suburb of Chilwell. He had arrived with his first wife Mary Cole and two children born in England and it would be several years later that events and circumstances would lead him to Ballarat. After the death of his first wife it was his union with Elizabeth Sparling that was to provide his second family and a daughter that was to marry George Edwin.

Regardless of earlier occupations all soon became miners in the search for riches. Later, Edward also progressed, with his occupation listed in the Black Hill rate book as 'Foreman, Goods Shed, Ballarat, Victoria'. Other records confirm that in 1888, Edward had been initiated into the England United Grand Lodge of Freemasons (Orion Lodge).

According to the 1905 electoral roll, in the year before his daughter's marriage, the Grant family lived at 239 Victoria Street, Ballarat East. The household lists EF (Edward Francis) as independent means, M (Maria Elizabeth) as home duties, EA (Elizabeth Agnes) and ME (Mary Elizabeth) as dressmakers, and a younger daughter Jessie. At the time of his daughter's marriage he nominates his occupation as 'gentleman' and the witnesses' signatures are Mary Elizabeth's half-brother and sister, William J Grant and Ethel A Grant.

Edna's maternal grandparents were also members of the Ballarat East fraternity and it is easy to speculate that her parents had known each other from childhood or certainly a long period before their marriage, given their proximity to local institutions and their homes.

Of course this was lives past for the children of the James family and they were known only as the older family members of today.

The industrial age

Like all communities following the industrial revolution in England and later in Europe, the combination of rail and steam became the major driver of the Victorian Period. In the Colony of Port Phillip (Victoria) the movement of people gathered pace as district after district announced another potential rush. The volume of immigrants that trod rough tracks soon saw roads and highways linking major centres.

By 1862 the steam train had linked Geelong and Ballarat to Melbourne and her ports. As in many major cities of the world, rail was opening up the country.

Yet the history of a birthplace or city is unknown to any small child and their demands are little more than the warmth of a swaddling rug and the smell and milk of their mother.

Of little interest to a newborn child are the affairs of State and community. In continental Europe, empires were in decline as voices for independence were now in full voice. Much had occurred after many years of wars and instability. In the United States of America at the century's turn, the War of Independence had long ago provided the Declaration of Independence and the American Constitution. The War Between the States (1861–65) was 50 years on. America was flexing her muscles in the world context as the old world powers struggled for new ideas.

Britain still ruled the world with her navy and dominions but was unprepared or blinded by the sun for a new world order. The time was early in the twentieth century as Australia was beginning its growth towards Nationhood. Less than a decade prior, the then sovereign states had come together to join as the Commonwealth of Australia. Federation had been agreed after much debate in 1900 and proclaimed on 1 January 1901. It was a time of much change as the James family commenced its generational growth in Victoria's major regional centre.

Those early years of the new century were ones of transition as the dynamics of life and country engulfed all those who made the cities and the far reaches their home. No matter the mix of the population, the majorities were from the shores of Britain and still maintained an allegiance to the English crown.

Edna's birth year, 1907, is a long time ago. A full century and some years, if succeeding generations care to count.

Ballarat, Birth, Family

Many changes, both within the broader world and Australia occurred in her lifetime, yet these changes are not in themselves any greater than the changes that occur over any one long life.

Those many years and there significance depend on many factors, outside your name, birthplace, and the economic status you are born into.

In Ballarat, the tide of people who swarmed to the city and outlying hills and gullies had long passed. Gold fever and the hope of riches that had brought thousands upon thousands to Ballarat had faded. Many had moved to the Western State of Australia as names like Coolgardie, Southern Cross and Kalgoorlie called some old and a new generation of prospectors. Unknown to the little girl in Ballarat her future husband's parents were part of that exodus and had settled in those far flung goldfields. Joseph Denman and his siblings were all born on the other side of the continent.

Life at home

Those who stayed in Ballarat were a different type of pioneer … community builders. Edna's dad, George Edwin, by all accounts was a large, capable man who like his father and many of his peers listed their early occupation as a miner. Much later he was to work as a bread carter for a long and established Baker's family business, Haynes Bread. George

Edwin had inherited the full bucket of the James genes which implied strong facial features, good looking without being handsome and approaching 5'9" (178 cm) in height.

Mary, Edna's mother, was the opposite. Whereas her husband had height and substance in his build, she would have been described as small and fine bodied. Later in her long life she was described by her youngest son's children as 'little nana'. In a few photos of their time, George Edwin possibly in the early years of his marriage can be seen with a centre part, dark brown wavy hair and a fine mustache to complement his wife's long light brown hair which she maintained through her life. In contrast, Mary gazes at the camera dressed in a long gathered skirt with a matching long-sleeved jacket. At her neck is a high ruffled blouse with coloured ribbon. She is the picture of the successful middle-class woman.

In her eighties, anyone who watched her morning ritual would observe the long flowing grey tresses held together and wound in a bun at the back of the head. All managed in place by long hairpins and a hairnet.

For Edna and her siblings, Ballarat East and its institutions were home, the gateway to Bridge Road and the main commercial centre bustling with its shops and entertainment. They had little knowledge of its past glory as the 'Golden City'.

Ballarat, Birth, Family

In Edna's early years, much like all small children, her life revolved around the home environment. George, older by some 15 months was not only her big brother but a mate who would share all of her formative years of home and school. Their early years would be remembered as an idyllic time of being underfoot in the kitchen with the smells of the house all about them.

The house in Stawell Street was a comfortable period home and would have stood out from the typical miner's cottage, clad in timber, with a sheet iron roof and wide front verandah. These miners' cottages were so portable that many were uprooted and taken away by their owners as they left for other destinations.

As outside toilets or privy (bucket) was the norm and tap water into the house was a luxury, much of the past by today's standards were primitive.

Never a mansion, 8 Stawell Street was certainly much higher up the social scale than the basic miner's cottage that was the mainstream of housing in East Ballarat.

In Edna's own words:

'When I was a small girl we lived in a four-roomed house, with no gas or electricity. Candles were used in the bedrooms and lamps in the other rooms. There was a verandah across the back two rooms which had a single tap. Dad made shelves and a tap where we washed the

dishes and clothes. We had our bath on Saturday night in a big tub in front of the fire. The water was heated in a large honey tin on top of the stove.'

Edna's first family home as a child, 2018

The four-roomed home would have provided two bedrooms, a sitting room and the hub of the house the kitchen. Here life revolved around the kitchen, cooking and preparing family meals. Vegetables could be purchased from the Chinese gardeners but most households grew their own staples. Eggs and milk were readily available with most families rearing chickens and fowls. Yet there is a suggestion of a little more comfort than the typical miners' cottage.

Ballarat, Birth, Family

The world beyond the property fence commenced with an unsealed road. It would have been dry and dusty in summer and wet and muddy in winter.

The seasons in Ballarat can be challenging even today and winter snow is not completely unknown. Today's modern insulated housing and gas central heating would have been a figment of imagination. All forms of heating and cooking were provided by burning wood and possibly coal. Every man, woman and child learned at an early age to set kindling and brush for the oven box or fireplace.

Stawell Street is part of a series of streets that align north towards Victoria Street and face the main Melbourne/Geelong Rail line. Divided by the rail track, Stawell Street continues its length past Scotts Parade adjoining Russell Square to bisect Humffray Street North and beyond the Yarrowee. Two blocks west, Queen Street parallels Stawell and provides the pedestrian and vehicle overpass north.

More than 100 years on, 8 Stawell Street still stands today, with little changes to its outside fascia. Number 8 and the adjacent block (10) were listed as part of Edna's grandfather's property holdings and rented by her parents. Her parents never owned property and continued to rent, moving to a larger home in Humffray Street when they needed more rooms and a little more luxury.

A growing family

Their new home in Humffray Street and its surrounds became the central point for the next 20 years. Rate books confirm the family moved to 295 Humffray Street North nearer to the environment that was to be so influential in Edna and her siblings' memories.

'Later we shifted into a bigger house that had six rooms and plenty of space for a garden. Dad always had a wonderful garden and grew all our vegetables. We had wonderful parents to help us and Dad was lots of fun and the games we all played, yet there was always something in need of doing ... Dad was working for Haynes Bakery as a carter and he was up early to start his round delivering bread and after work wood had to be chopped for the oven as well as mending boots and looking after the horse.

Mum made all our clothes and prepared our meals. She baked, made jams and pickles and that is where I learned to cook. On Sundays we all went to church and Sunday school and later us kids went up to Black Hill to explore. We had to cross the creek and climb over the brick making site to reach the hill. There was a chalk tunnel that you had to crawl on your knees some of the way up to the top where we built a little shelter.

The Black Hill lookout could be seen from the back fence and much of the land from the old diggings. Close by was the paddock where Dad kept the horse.'

Ballarat East was the oldest area of the two municipalities, a legacy of the mining districts of Ballarat East and Nerrina. A community of strong-willed individuals and activity that reflected its working class character.

The 'East' was the first to gain municipal status along with its growing institutions, the town hall, library, fire station and secondary college.

No modern journey from the State capital via the Western Freeway to Ballarat will resist the fall of the road from Woodman's Hill onto the wide expanse of Victoria Street to bypass the Bridge Street Mall as the city unfolds. Of course that was not the city of yesterday and the pathway west was somewhat different.

A changing city

With the turn of the twentieth century and the addition of another decade, the vibrancy and glitter that saw the Golden City rise to unprecedented heights had waned.

Gold was still being mined, but this was now a very different city and other industries were replacing the decades of mining. All through this period, the residents of Ballarat East, regardless of how they measured success, were disadvantaged by the geographical location of their city. It was to be many years before the amalgamation of both municipalities.

> **18 August 1905, first electric tram service from the Wendouree depot and terminating in Victoria Street at Stawell Street.**

Still, the legacy of earlier days and wealth could be seen in the proliferation of the West's major public buildings, monuments and wide divided central street (Sturt Street) with rotundas and statues to commemorate empire and glory. Statues to Queen Victoria, the Irish poet Robert Burns and Thomas Moore were all symbols of civic pride. The impact of British life and obligation to the Crown was inherent in most of the population.

On the day of her birth, Sunday 4 August, only the stamp of the few remaining mines' ore crushers resounded over the city. The cry of 'gold' had ceased but deep mining still accounted for much of the State's revenue. Within a decade the last mine would cease.

The population went about its Sunday morning rituals; the bustle around the kitchen as large kettles filled to the brim heated water for the bath. In his authorised biography, the great English fast bowler Harold Larwood (b.1904) recalls 'scrubbing himself at home in front of the fire in the same cramped tin bath that his father had used before'. Larwood's father was a coal miner and for a period after leaving school, so was Larwood.

Ballarat, Birth, Family

Although the workers of Ballarat were not coal miners there is little to distinguish between the grime of coal dust and the grime of earth and mud. The universality of the period shows the common lot of the miner and the working class, whether in Nottinghamshire or Ballarat East.

Best clothes being readied for church. Boots and shoes brightened for the day after the weekly grind of dust and grime. Hats and bonnets adjusted to the fashion as few members of the faith went bare headed. Hats were part of the established Edwardian dress code. In the preceding years women's clothes were rich and elegant covering from neck to below the knee. The vogue according to the Buckley & Nunn's mail-order catalogue was for blouses of laces, beads, pleats and frills. The working man continued to wear moleskin trousers, flannel shirts and boots, but on the Sabbath would be seen in a smart suit with a stiff collar and a waistcoat.

Outside, if you were of means, the sulky would be readied for its Sunday outing or it was 'shanks pony' … you walked. The practice of worship was part of the community and family lifestyle. Near at hand in Humffray Street North the local Methodist Church waited each Sunday with open doors. Far in the distant City the crown of the Town Hall and spires of St Patrick's Cathedral and St Peter's could just be seen in the west.

Equally impressive was the Ballarat Station building, Craig's Hotel and the commercial hub along Lydiard Street.

Despite an increase in mechanisation and the motor car, the working horse was still a common sight on the streets and byways. The streets were not yet sealed and in summer months required continuous watering in the attempt to smother the dust. The horse trams which serviced the West were being replaced by electric trams and the progress of electric lighting and gas supplied to the Lydiard and Sturt Street commercial centres and housing was impacting the wider community.

It's a relatively easy task to represent the formal information of the beginning of life from the records of Government documents. It is a harder task to fashion and shape the growth of a person with their personality and relationships. To do this you would need to know the woman and maybe it's only fitting that a son might attempt to tell the story with the understanding that much of her early life is conjecture and much more her own words shared in the final years of her life. Nevertheless, it is a story worth telling for her grandchild and great grandchildren.

Childhood days

Children of the early nineteenth century were to some degree free spirits without the restrictions or fear of modern day temptations or horrors. Assuming that a child of the times was part of a strong family with a roof and regular income, much entertainment was to hand.

Ballarat, Birth, Family

Looking after your children and early learning was part of the parental role with hopefully a nearby grandparent. Childminding facilities or kindergarten services were unheard of except for those who were exceptionally rich and could afford a governess.

Like many cities, Ballarat has long had a history of poverty against its glittering wealth. Established in 1865, the Ballarat District Orphan Asylum (renamed the Ballarat Orphanage in 1909) was built to house and care for children separated from their parents by circumstances and poverty. With local community support the foundling home and adjacent farm are an inherent part of the Golden City's story. In a much later time, a black history was to emerge that was to bring deep-seated shame on the Orphanage and other Church-based institutions.

Located in Victoria Street, the Orphanage and its residents were an immediate neighbour of the James household in Stawell Street. Never mentioned in his lifetime and either regarded as uninteresting or secret was a year spent within those high walls by her future husband. Stranger still, that two lives in such close proximity were never to meet as children, yet by location were only separated by high walls and some 500 metres.

If a generation of males had signed their occupation as 'miner', succeeding generations of the James/Grant women had supported their husbands and families with their sewing skills. Unknown to the present generation was the impact of the treadle sewing machine on each life but the skills of needle and thread were very much apparent. Passed from mother to daughter was the skill of making clothes for the family's use and occasional profit. Edna's mother Mary and her sister Jessie Grant were recorded in a succession of Census by occupation as seamstresses.

The quality of hand stitching could now be complemented by the speed of the sewing machine. The 'Singer' operated by a foot pedal had an array of functions from stitching to embroidery. Still much was to occur before the little girl commenced an apprenticeship.

Early childhood can quickly recede with the learning of sounds and words and the impact of any immediate surrounds. By the age of four a new baby was on the way and George had started school. Days were spent following her mother in and around the house but mainly in the central hub of the kitchen. Here was every woman's workstation, with the heat of the wood stove and the glow of the oven's fire box.

Each meal was prepared on the large wooden table, from stews or casseroles of the day to homemade biscuits and cakes. Tea was the national drink and the kettle was always simmering on the stove. Electricity was not yet in the homes of Ballarat East so ironing clothes was done by heavy flat irons which had to be heated on the top of the stove.

Ballarat, Birth, Family

Washing clothes was a major task that required heating water in a tub and rubbing/scrubbing with homemade or velvet soap. The role and skills of the Victorian women were well entrenched in the psyche of the English/Australian community.

Girls from an early age helped their mother in every aspect of the home.

They learned to fold clothes, peel potatoes, strip peas from the pods and all manner of helpful tasks. It was in this environment that the little girl first sprinkled flour and learnt to knead pastry. Scones and Cornish pasties were the mainstay of the family.

Of course there was time to play outside the house and she recalled many adventures with George as well as playing hopscotch, drop the handkerchief, oranges and lemons, and skip rope (Skippy). Other games played at school included spinning tops. Edna recalled that her dad had made tops for both her and George.

'They were just a tapered piece of wood with a cut down nail fixed at the end and of course, a length of string to spin the top with. We had great parents who always had time for us and although we didn't have a lot of money made a very happy life.'

Besides these and other games the family now had another son and brother. Norman Wellesley had been born in late

1911. Who he was named after is problematic, with his mother diverting from the usual precedent for males, named for their father or grandfathers. His eldest brother named for his father yet Norm was surprisingly not named for his maternal grandfather. Norm's middle name is somewhat unique and possibly resounds to the drum of Arthur Wellesley, the First Duke of Wellington.

New names and ideas were shaping the times.

CHAPTER 2

School Days

There is much conjecture as to how any young girl or child is prepared for school and life beyond the home. Parents have provided the basic speaking blocks of words and sounds and with an older brother to follow, school was soon to be Edna's next step. Edna at school age is showing signs of a gangly child, tall with long hair as dark as night.

> *'She had a thin awkward figure, a sallow skin without colour, dank dark hair and strong features ... so much for her person.'*
> *Northanger Abbey*, **Jane Austin**

Dressed in the period of the day would see clothes made from the latest dress catalogues by her mother. From their Stawell Street home, the Queen Street Primary School was only a matter of blocks and within easy walking distance. This little school that was the starting point for Edna's education is long gone and today is utilised as a community health and welfare centre.

Undoubtedly accompanied by her big brother, the first school day would surely combine both excitement and a little uncertainty.

School is a significant event for all families where a child takes their first steps away from the security of home into the wider world. For many a child it is a traumatic experience, but Edna was blessed with a chaperone, her brother George.

A couple of grades ahead, it was George who literally took her by the hand and provided that ingredient of safety, and later the occasional mischief. Edna was to meet new classmates and new teachers. In her later years, she remembered routines and timelines that were not like home.

'In those days, Monday morning was somewhat formal with the raising of the flag and the oath of allegiance to the monarch. We had to sing, 'God save our gracious King'. My brother George played the bugle while two other boys drummed, one on the kettle drum and the other on the base.'

School Days

Still, she survived and grew and in later years was to follow in George's footsteps as she guided her little brother on his first school day outing. With four years separating them, Norman would have been starting school in Edna's higher class years. It's possible given the age difference George, Edna and Norman all attended Queen Street together for a year. Later her youngest brother was to follow, although no complete school records were held at the Ballarat Historical society, John Leslie James (ref: 1/1083) is recorded on the 1921 student list.

The Queen Street Primary School was located on the corner of Dytes Parade and Queen Street. According to the Education Department's 1973 publication *Vision & Realisation Vol 2: a centenary history of state education in Victoria*, it originated as a free Presbyterian church school in 1863 and applied to become a State School in 1873.

The government of Victoria had long advanced education for all children in denomination schools. Much had been invested in the subjects to be taught. Supplied with the 'Little reader' series of the day, the 'three Rs' were the building blocks of education. Primary school was divided into five classes, with the average age of students starting school about six or seven, while the fifth class ages ranged up to 12 or 13.

The core subjects taught included:

- First class – reading, writing and arithmetic, ABC and monosyllables, copy single letters from the blackboard, addition and subtraction tables, repeat from memory easy rhymes
- Second class – reading, writing, arithmetic, grammar and geography, additionally girls were able to sew little
- Third class – reading, writing, arithmetic, grammar and geography
- Fourth class – higher level of reading, writing, arithmetic, grammar and geography
- Fifth class – maximise reading, writing, arithmetic, grammar and geography.

As Edna recalls:

'Such a long time ago but of course we had some homework and lessons from the series of readers. That was where we learnt dictation, composition and sums and I suppose history. It was the same book from the time George started and used by us all including Johnnie. We also had to learn our arithmetic tables at night to be checked with our parents.'

Along with the little blue reader, school was a mixture of chalk and slate and 'Victorian age' discipline. Looking back on her school years Edna felt they passed all too quickly and except for a few friends they blurred into endless periods of activities that prepared girls for life as a homemaker or occupations fitted for women. She remembered school outings too:

'School picnics were great, we went to Lake Wendouree by vans and went across the lake on a paddle steamer, followed by rides and games on the lawns.'

Edna, in her own words, was 'not a good scholar' but the bedrock of home studies and life skills were well placed for the future.

The First World War

At home, the family dynamics had changed. George was helping her father and looking for work and Norman was progressing through primary school, while the youngest member of the family was demanding attention. John Leslie James most probably named for his paternal grandfather had been born in 1915 in the second year of what was to be remembered as the Great War.

The First World War commenced on 18 July 1914.

This was the war to end all wars as it was later to be described. Names like Gallipoli and Lone Pine, Amiens and the Somme would soon be etched into the nation's consciousness as their boys enlisted for King and Country. Soon the AIF's casualty list from far away conflicts began to make their mark on the Australian community. Ballarat's sons were among them and years of fighting were still to come. Other than contemporary stories, the thoughts of most children would be relatively untouched except where a neighbour was seen in uniform or spoken about in whispers. Church services would include prayers for the troops and special mention of church members who were fighting.

Throughout this period every child would understand that something was different in their street. The war effort impacted every community with voluntary organisations raising money for the war and to help the troops. Women played their part in factories and by knitting for the troops, everything from socks to balaclavas. The grey sock instruction booklet for knitting socks was freely available. In schools across the land, children were doing their part. Edna along with other children was involved in writing letters to the troops to send along with parcels of socks and preserves.

Surprisingly, among her mother's keepsakes was a return letter to her daughter from the trenches of France, dated July 1918.

Stranger than fiction, the response was from Private John Stanley James 5429, Tenth Infantry Division AIF who was Edna's cousin, the eldest son of her uncle John Alfred.

They had never met.

School Days

Dear Edna,

Received your most welcome letter yesterday therefore it affords me great pleasure in answering same. I was surprised to get it, in fact I got quite a shock as I haven't had a letter for some weeks and it is difficult to imagine that you are attending the same school as I had. Let us hope you make a better job than me. I have never had the pleasure of seeing you but hope to one day. At present we are in the trenches of the Huns and they do not like the Australians because we are a bit too good. He sends over his usual song of hate daily but we give him his full iron ration.

You must be a clever little girl to write such a lovely letter. You can't be much more than 10 years of age but of course you come from a clever family. If you can write again we like to know someone is thinking of us at the following address. Pte. James JS. 5429.

10th Infantry, care of the Australian Imperial Force, France.

Please remember me to your father and mother also brother.

I am yours respectively,
J.S. James

> **25 April 1916, celebration of first Anzac Day in Australia.**

Girls' school and beyond

Post primary school, Edna attended a girls' school, before seeking work as an apprentice. She related the following memories of that time of significant growth and change:

'Later I attended the girls' school, after finishing the seventh grade. It was for girls only and was at the back of the library in Barkley Street. I had to walk down from Humffray Street and Russell Square across to Queen Street and cut into Victoria Street as far down as the synagogue. I can't think of the street that led to Barkley Street but it was at the side of the library and the East Fire Brigade station.

The lessons there were much the same as the State school, ordinary work, arithmetic, sewing, darning and cooking and all that, and we made meals that the teachers could eat. We learned to make scones and little buns, pasties and stews, there were about 20 girls and we worked in pairs. Someone would be mixing the flour, someone rolling the paste, someone else cutting the meat and peeling vegetables, we all had something to do. Then each item was placed in the oven and cooked.

Our other main jobs was to wash all the pots and cutlery and our work clothes and pinafore and stuff.

School Days

We all wore aprons and hats when we cooked and after cooking we washed them in a tub with cakes of soap and a washboard. After that we were taught how to iron with those big flat irons that were heated on top of the wood stoves. I remember that I got a burn on my arm when I was testing it one day but it just stung for a little while.

I had to get up about seven as it took about half an hour to walk to school. Lunch was made by Mum until I was about 13, then I made it myself. It was mainly bread and jam or bread and cheese and sometimes a slice of German sausage or a bacon and egg slice that Mum made. We always had a piece of cake.

During the school breaks I played rounders and there was tennis but we couldn't afford that. There was also swimming but I wasn't allowed to do that. Mum wouldn't let me.

Spanish influenza epidemic – Ballarat 1918–1919.

After leaving the girls' school, Dad had spoken to Mr Young about an apprenticeship but there were no vacancies. He told Dad that we had to wait until the forewoman advanced another apprentice to the next level. So I went and served in a baby shop for a couple of months. I worked with Mrs Kerner in Bridge Road and I served in the shop and sold baby things and learned to repair umbrellas. We covered them and replaced broken ribs.

That lasted about three months and then I went to Lucas's in Doveton Street and they put me pressing nighties and underwear and then I had to put French knots in nighties and little rows of tucks. The Lucas *factory was in Doveton Street and I used to walk or occasionally take the bus. Most of the girls had bikes during my time. That was where I met Kitty. She worked in the office and later her sister Daisy did too. We became great mates.*

I stayed there until the apprenticeship came up. Mr. Young's tailor shop was in Bridge Street before moving to Sturt Street later on. He had a good business, but he drank, a man who would do well in a circus; he was big, but not fat and always wore a beautiful grey suit. He had two travellers who went to Dimboola, Mildura and Stawell and all around and then he had two vest hands, three trouser hands and four or five others.

When I started he must have had about 10 working for him. It was the days before suits were bought off the hook. First I had to learn how to use a tailor's thimble as they don't have a top like an ordinary one. They taped your finger down next to the knuckle so you learnt to use the side not the top and you are taught to use only little stitches. You advance to small pieces of material as suits were all hand sewn. The apprentices do the padding of the coats and when they get to the level of an improver you would do the basting of the coat.

They would soak the canvas which had already been pressed and shrunk before its use and tack a type of horsehair inside the shoulders to give it shape. Then it would be tacked in white cotton with each stitch a quarter of an inch apart (1 cm). There was a lot to learn.

To put the shape into a coat, you made the pockets and padded them, sometimes with a flap on the pocket, some coats had three pockets, two on the right side and one on the other. In a lot of cases they had a little buttonhole on the two breast pockets.

There were three apprentices after me and I was the improver and our room was upstairs and the presser was downstairs. One day I fell down the stairs, plonk, plonk, holding an iron and didn't get a scratch! At that time, an apprenticeship was four years and you became skilled in coats, vests and trousers as well as pressing the finished suit. You were bound for four years, but some didn't last the distance. We were paid only seven and sixpence. I had finished my apprenticeship when the Depression came and the boss put the prices down but there was no work.'

Opportunity is such a wonderful word with its connotation of change and possible advancement yet without sufficient income most children of the day were headed directly from school to some form of employment. It was usual for this generation to commence work at 14 years of age.

> **'At fifteen her appearance is mending and she begins to alter her hair, her complexion improves, her features soften, her eyes gain more animation and her figure of more consequence.'**
> ***Northanger Abbey*, Jane Austin**

A university education was expensive and mainly reserved for males. For women of the day the roles were limited to nursing, apprenticeships, process working or the office. The social understanding was that this period was the preliminary to either marriage or homemaker.

Changing roles

As Edna commenced her apprenticeship, the family's home lives were now consolidated in the post-war period. Her eldest brother George had earlier started work at George Crocker's Drapery Pty Ltd, and Norman and John continued their school education. Not all work without the occasional fun as her youngest brother remembered helping their father on the delivery round. Obviously not for girls but Edna remembers that George always went with his father on a Saturday but was unsure if it was delivering bread or chopping and carting wood. Looking back when in his mid-80s, John was more specific.

'The bloody horse steered a course down the middle of the road as Dad went to customers on one side of the street and I chased up others on the opposite. It knew the round without any help from Dad and only increased its walking pace as the thought of oats crossed its mind. It was great fun.'

Not long after this period the first of the family patriarchs was to pass on. JJ died in 1923, leaving a void in the older generations' lives and for the younger members, the confusion of loss and death. John and Elizabeth Jane had been highly visible presences in the younger generation's lives especially George and Edna as the oldest grandchildren residing in Ballarat.

She remembered Grandpa's shop was nearby in Humffray Street and they also had a cart and delivered milk.

School Days

'They had cows and a little shed beside the shop as well as chooks and horses. Grandpa had a very successful business not far from their magnificent brick Edwardian home.'

216 Humffray St North, Ballarat East

Site of JJ's Grocer Shop, 2018

Extract from the *Ballarat Courier*, Monday 25 June 1932

On 24th June at his residence, 216 Humffray Street North, Ballarat East, John, dearly beloved husband of Elizabeth Jane and loving father of William (WA) John (deceased) and George and Ethel (Mrs. F Larkin) died aged 83.

A letter written by George to his mother dated December 31 1911 from his grandparent's residence at 216 Humffray Street still survives. Whether a coincidence or not, the date of the letter is the birthdate of Norman James. Edna's grandparents are minding the children.

Dear Mother,
I am just writing you a few lines to let you know how I am getting on well and enjoying myself very much and I hope you have enjoyed yourself to. I think that Grandma is going to take us to Bunningyong on New Year's day. I hope it is a nice day …
I have nothing more to say.
So goodbye dear Mother, your loving baby boy,
Gorgie James
God is love
Family – Family

Edna's two uncles had previously moved from Ballarat, John Alfred to Wangaratta and Uncle Bill to Western Australia. Before going west, William Henry had married Alice Franklin and moved to Kaniva. John had also married a Ballarat girl and had eight children, some which were to

School Days

play a part in Edna's life beyond Ballarat. Tragically, John Alfred died a year before his father (1922) at age 54. Uncle John, his wife Nellie and their children had been frequent holiday visitors to Edna's parents' home. Edna recalled that her parents 'held an open house' and all were welcome.

'Imagine all us kids sharing beds and talking all through the night. Their visits were very happy times.'

After Grandpa's death, Grandma James continued to live at home. Her daughter and husband have moved into 216 Humffray to continue her care. They combine this activity with their new business, as they had recently opened a grocery store in Victoria Street. Nearly a century later, this Edwardian home hides behind its high surrounding fence and overhanging foliage.

It remains the last visible legacy of a James generation linked to Edna and Ballarat's past.

Entering through the gate, you confront its wide sweeping verandah that surrounds the house and shades the ornate lead glass door. Inside, the passage leads to high roofed ceiling rooms with little change from an earlier century. Today the sound of a family gathering has been replaced with the business of care and its role of Ballarat Community Health.

In words of the great American
singer-songwriter Bob Dylan …
'Times they are a-Changing'.

A vibrant city

Continuing change is now part of the immediate future. Australia, like many other countries, had moved on after the war and change could be seen in every street. Fashion and entertainment progressed rapidly along with home conveniences. The electric light, radio and telephones were now embraced by the major cities. Outside the family's singalong and the pleasure in peddling the pianola, the self-playing piano that read rolls of scripted music, the options were many.

Unlike his sister and younger brother, it seems Norm never touched the keys of a piano. John, or Jessie as he was called by his friends, was to engage the world thereafter wherever a piano was in sight. The youngest member of the family took to the ivories and became an accomplished player. Edna recalled an incident from their childhood where John was badly scolded by boiling water at the foot of his mother. Curtailed from school for many weeks he learnt each key and scale by ear under the tuition of his mother. Such was his skill, John, would hold centre stage, providing endless entertainment for family and the friends that shared his rich social life.

Nearer home, the twin towns had merged into the greater City of Ballarat and electric trams and city lighting part of daily life. Australians embraced the motor car and further changes were occurring rapidly. From the early 1920s, the

School Days

North American car company assembled cars in Geelong, the 1908 and the Ford Model T, and others followed. As it is today, the car became the image of success and freedom.

Ballarat was blessed with many a distraction when it came to social activities – a dip at the Eureka Stockade pool, a steamer ride across Lake Wendouree and a number of theatres which opened to packed crowds on Friday and Saturday nights. Vaudeville and pantomime were a staple part of community entertainment with their roots from the 'old country' and Europe. Ballarat had long had a history of stage and dance and the older generation would still raise a smirk at the publicity and crowds who adored Lola Montez and her interpretive sexual spider dance routines. Soon to be an institution in Ballarat, the South Street competitions were renowned across the Eastern States. Events and competitions staged at the Coliseum could hold an audience of 8000 with competitors and patrons from home and interstate. Annual contests included eisteddfod, elocution, singing and bands. The Australian Band Championship was launched as part of the South Street Competitions. Marching and quickstep competitions were held at the City Oval. Such was the success of its operatic singing competition that the Melbourne paper initiated the Sun Aria for emerging singers with a large monitory prize.

Edna and her friends enjoyed many a performance as well as community singing programs run for the public. Many of the songs of this day became her favourites, among them 'Good night Irene', 'Good night sweetheart', 'Over the rainbow', 'Walking my baby back home' and 'Three little words'.

With the coming of film, Ballarat was reported in the local paper 'as gone mad on amusements'. Every night 10–20,000 are said to be at the pictures, with another 2000 at live shows, socials or dancing.

Along Sturt and Lydiard streets the posters and billboards called patrons to the talkies as the days of silent film lost their appeal. The brilliance of Charlie Chaplin's 'Little Tramp' and the host of silent stars from John Barrymore to Dolores Costello faded for a new generation.

In 1927, *The Jazz Singer* ushered in the marvel of voice and images. New Hollywood stars shone out as glamour and sound drew crowds from the street. Competition among the theatres was considerable, seeking the locals' patronage. The Britannia, Regent, Plaza and Majestic all shone brightly with matinees and evening screenings.

Picture nights were soon to be a staple part of Ballarat's social life and Edna and her brothers joined the wider population, dazzled by the flickering images. Soon the new world was ushering in a toe-tapping sound that energised the mood of the next generation. The thirties had ushered in the jazz years with the sound of the horn and the honky-tonk piano that reputedly took Australia by storm. It must

School Days

have had their feet tapping as the crowds surged to a new sound.

America introduced jazz, and it soon swept the world with its sound. Yet Ballarat East was far from the clubs of New York and Chicago and the weekly Saturday social dances were soon to replace the local community social barn dances. Somewhat distanced in time was the recollection that Norman, Edna's brother, romanced his future wife under the silver screen rather than to the steps and whirls of the waltz or the Albert's quadrille.

Sport, always a part of the Australian self-image, drew massive crowds throughout the country. Horseracing and betting was a definitive part of the Australian psyche. Locally, every country city had their own cup carnival and although overshadowed by the Melbourne Cup, it was part of the community's social calendar. Dowling Forrest was the site of the first Victorian Amateur Turf Club in 1895 before transferring its meetings to Caulfield in Melbourne. In Ballarat and Victoria the dominant football code was Australian Rules and this separated the southern states from New South Wales and Queensland which held fast to the English stalwart of rugby. Yet football does not seem to have been a family staple.

Whether the family or the brothers ever ventured to the Eastern Oval to support the Red and White Imperials is another lost memory, although within comfortable walking distance and surely Edna's younger brothers' peer group and workmates must have plied the suggestion a time or two. Down Humffray Street to the rail line, past the pub and turn into Scotts Parade and the oval is in view. Without a car in the family the options of transport other than the tram network was by bicycle or foot. Many leather soles were replaced to save a three penny fare.

Edna recollected that George had joined the Golden Point Tennis Club and was a ranked player in his division. John was learning the art of 'off spin' and winning matches for the local church cricket competition. In later life he was to grace the greens as a fine lawn bowler for various suburban clubs. Norm's sporting involvements are somewhat clouded with other interests as his circle of friends widened.

Among his close friends was David (Dave) Desnoy. Where they initially met is unclear but probably they commenced their apprenticeship as painters together before Dave joined the regular army for a three year stint at age 18. Except for George, all the James children had become indentured apprentices.

Near at hand, the wide expanses of Russell Square loomed large (approximately 18 acres). Bordered by Stawell Street on the west, Humffray Street North and Haymes Street on the east, this sea of green extended its length to Scotts Parade. Possibly based on the English common it was surrounded by large oak trees that shaded the rustic outer pathways that ringed the square. Today, the multiple sporting ovals through its length are the home of various community sporting associations with clubrooms and amenities.

Branching out

Edna, in earlier conversations, related that her parents would not let her attend dances until she was 18, yet it's reasonable to suspect that in keeping with that dictate she was able to accompany her brother George to the odd function. At 18, Edna is now part of a working family and socialising with a wider group beyond the church community. In the relatively short time at the Lucas factory she had made a new group of friends. These friendships continued long after she commenced her apprenticeship and later became part of the dance crowd.

As in many country locations and cities there are workplaces that become institutions and the Lucas factory was one of these. In *The Golden Thread: the story of a fashion house*, the story of the rise and determination of a widow to support her four children unfolds.

From a backroom workshop in 1888, she sought orders of 'white work' from the town drapers. Elle, like Edna, had left school at age 14 and created an industry that provided much needed employment for women. She not only provided work but encouraged a work family culture soon known as the 'busy bees'.

With the help of her eldest son they expanded to a two acre site in Doveton Street after the collapse of the Phoenix foundry. She understood and practised employee relations long before the invention of Human Resource Departments and became a leading light in fabrics design and fashion. Long before modern entrepreneurs, the Lucas girls and company were pivotal in many community activities, including helping to fund Ballarat's WW1 Avenue of Honour. This long tree-lined avenue is a tribute to the fallen soldiers by the Ballarat community.

CHAPTER 3

The Great Depression at the Door

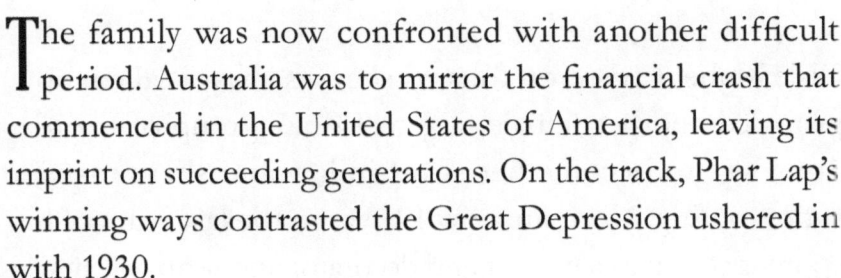

The family was now confronted with another difficult period. Australia was to mirror the financial crash that commenced in the United States of America, leaving its imprint on succeeding generations. On the track, Phar Lap's winning ways contrasted the Great Depression ushered in with 1930.

Coming late to Australia, the collapse of the American financial system brought worldwide devastation. Companies and industries soon began reduced working hours before layoffs and then closure spread near to home. By 1933, a quarter of the population was unemployed. Ballarat's citizens were no exception. It had an immediate impact on the family.

This second generation of young Australians was to undergo countless challenges. With no money on offer, much of the big city population headed to the bush seeking work and a feed in the rural areas. Many relocated to labour in the Government's public works programs including the construction of the Great Ocean Road.

> **1933: Ballarat's unemployed rate peaked at about 27%**

The James family, like the rest of Australia, was caught in the Depression. Work had replaced school and teenagers had become adults. George at 25 had consolidated his position at Crocker's and had met and would soon propose to his future wife.

Elsie Mabel Parker, or Tous, as she was always called, now provided another female face to Edna's group of friends. Tous was to become her sister-in-law and share many a future outing. Norman, now 19, was in the last years of his apprenticeship as a painter and decorator and John was newly engaged as an apprentice pastrycook. The Bridge Street shops had become a ghost town and suits were not in high demand. Edna's boss started a 'last on … first off' strategy before closing the business. Edna remembered doing some odd jobs and housekeeping before her father was let go from Haynes Bakery. Both Norm and John joined Edna

The Great Depression at the Door

at home as with little work, both were also retrenched. To qualify for 'Susso' or government relief, no member of the family unit could be earning an income.

With George still working with reduced hours this disqualified the family from any government support. Edna remembers her father's anger at a suggestion to move George on to enable relief. 'No son of mine will go without,' was his answer.

For a brief period George's pay at Crocker's was the only income. Yet they all survived the shared hardships to see out the next decade. During this period as the family settled into the Depression years, Edna's father had somehow or other garnered sufficient funds to set himself up as an independent carter.

Unknown as the source, yet suspected as a loan from his mother, George Edwin slowly began to change the family's fortunes. Bread could be bought from independent bakers and on-sold as his home service brought new and older customers. Complimenting this activity both his wife and daughter had set to with a cottage style industry of dressmaking and alterations. They were to successfully ply this trade and supplement the family income long after the Depression years had gone.

During this period, governments encouraged the unemployed to prospect for gold. The gold price rose, so the long-neglected

Victorian goldfields energised for a short period. Edna's brother Norm and his mate Dave took to prospecting reviving the long held occupation of previous generations. According to his sister, their claim was thought to be at the rear of the Humffray Street property and the adjoining Yarrowee River. Their efforts remembered by all yielded a little colour and described at the time as a golden nugget valued at 25 pounds. Sufficient to enable both families much needed succour.

Coming out the other side

Yet, like all communities during and after the Depression, life had not entirely stopped. Participation in sport and watching sport is part of the Australian psyche and parallels history with most major Australian events. In the thirties, there was racing's Phar Lap and Big Red, the feats of Don Bradman and the Bodyline series in the test arenas, and the exploits of Jack Crawford and Harry Hopman as tennis greats.

Nearer home, Edna in her conversations at age 87 smiled recalling long remembered events of a particular Boxing Day picnic where three families celebrated together (most likely uncles, aunts and cousins).

'We were over the Depression and had managing to get by. We caught the little train to Bunningyong taking all our food with us. Some of us younger ones climbed the mountain and then we all played cricket.

The Great Depression at the Door

On New Year's Day the three families went by motor-coach to Lake Learmonth, played cricket again and fished and paddled in the water. The older folk went for walks and prepared our meals, each family brought something which was shared. They were very happy days.'

With JJ's passing, their paternal grandmother Elizabeth Jane was to enjoy another decade of life in time to see her eldest grandson married. In February 1935, George Fredrick married Tous (Elsie) Parkes in the Golden Point Church. George was 29 years old and together they saw rays of sunshine in their future. At the groom's request, his sister's signature is one of the witnesses on the wedding certificate. In terms of celebration, the wedding was the highlight after the past coming of age. Both Edna and Norman had celebrated their 21st birthdays and John was nearing his majority.

A photo of Edna records the image of a confident young woman posing in a full length gown with an embroidered bodice and fashionable shoes. Her hair is now cut short and styled to portray the modern woman. Bobbed and then shingled hair became popular and short hair produced the cloche hat which dominated hat fashion for the next half decade. The roaring twenties of 'flappers', brought short skirts and loose stylised garments, with Berlei selling one-piece undergarments with suspender belts and stockings. Woman's fashion and beauty tips were now driven by Hollywood leading ladies like Claudette Colbert, Barbara Stanwyck and Bette Davis.

Yet for the generation who made their own clothes, the pattern books and journals of fashion magazines were widely available. By the 1930s, an independent women could buy coloured leather shoes, open-toed sandals and rayon stockings.

In conversations with John, long after his retirement, he related that his sister was a terrific dancer. Photos of the pair doesn't confirm his statements but they do show them together attending wedding functions and outings. Edna now in her mid-twenties was a regular at Saturday night dances along with a group of women who became lifelong friends. Many worked at the Lucas factory, a major employee of women in Ballarat. A few were secretaries or plied their trade at the Myer Woolen Mill in North Ballarat. Most were to meet their prospective husbands at these Saturday dances with options of the Town Hall, St Patrick's and the Railway Institute.

It was the big band era, established during the war years, and the local bands played the music of swing, echoing Tommy Dorsey, Glen Miller and Harry James.

Brother and sister

John, Edna, Edna Brown and Norm

Always Something More To Do

Kitty, Daisy, Edna Brown, Ada and Clarice made up the gang as they plied the dance floor. This group travelled far and wide with boyfriends and suitors, including Melbourne jaunts and coastal holidays. Photos of the group show escapades including bush picnics and posing with croquet sticks. It is obvious to the eye that there is bond between them all and for Edna, days of pleasure. The first to separate from the group was Clarice who had along with Edna met an interesting young man from the fire station. Edna, after a brief romance, moved on. Mick Sparkman was soon part of the gang and shortly after proposed to Clarice and was accepted. They were to marry within the year and Edna sparkled as the maid of honour. Edna Brown followed leaving the remainder to a quieter beat.

Girls at play

The Great Depression at the Door

During this post-Depression period, Edna had never returned to full-time work, as her parents' neared retirement and her mother suffered occasional bouts of depression. According to the local rate books, the family moved to a smaller house at 136 Humffray Street with her father now enjoying retirement. Edna was now the de facto head of household and provider. She ran the house and continued with dressmaking and alterations, making vests at home for a city tailor.

Still, there was time to see the odd movie and Edna's favourite actor was at his height. Robert Taylor had become a Hollywood leading man starring in *Camille*, *A Magnificent Obsession*, *A Yankee in Oxford* and many more. She met Kit regularly in the city's tea houses and they were equally comfortable in each other's home. With the family now fully grown, independence is knocking on a new decade's door.

Clarice Sparkman's wedding day

Norm has completed his apprenticeship and is working locally as a painter. John after working for a period at Portland as a pastrycook was looking to return home and then move to Melbourne.

Within the year their maternal grandmother, Elizabeth Jane, had died leaving her family fortune to the care of her daughter, Auntie Ethel.

Much was to change, again and again in the following years. JJ's will was simply structured leaving equal parts to his surviving children (John Alfred was deceased) and the Edwardian house and all the properties to his wife for the duration of her comfort and life. Elizabeth Jane's will and testament is unknown and George Edwin's share somehow slipped from his grasp and was lost to his family.

The Second World War

The world now recovered from past major events had settled into a new cycle. Beyond the reach of the English Empire, clouds of Fascists were tainting European skies. The Spanish civil war had been raging since 1936 and Abyssinia invaded by Italy a year earlier. The Empire was still entrenched in Australia, and this generation understood the threat and losses of war. In every town and city across Australia 'Lest we forget' was enshrined in monuments and plaques.

In September 1939, the Australian Prime Minister Robert Menzies delivered the fateful news: 'My fellow Australians, it is my melancholy duty to advise the nation that Great Britain has declared war with Germany and as such Australia is also at war.'

The offspring of George Edwin and Mary are full grown and fit the James profile. Norm physically takes after both his brother George and his father. All are well proportioned and about 5 foot 9 inches in imperial measurements. John has leapfrogged both his brothers and levelled out to a Collingwood six-footer, around 181 cm. Edna is slender and slightly taller than the woman of the day.

Around this time, Norm probably met his future wife. Edith Gwendoline Fraser, or Gwen as she preferred, was a local girl from Ballarat South and another of the Lucas Girls. Gwen worked as both a yarn spinner and inspector. She was a future catch. Another potential sister-in law was in the making.

Kitty, Edna, Gwen & Tous

Along with Norm, his younger brother John had romanced and won an eligible young lady and they were soon engaged to be married. Ethel Grace Montgomery was born beyond the boundaries of Ballarat and when they met was working for a family in Ballarat city. In early 1940, John left for Melbourne with the offer of more permanent work and for a short period resided in Grey Street, St Kilda. Grace

The Great Depression at the Door

followed soon after and found suitable work near at hand. John related many stories of the long early morning bike ride between his premises in St Kilda to his workplace across town. In past chats, he smiled and rolled his eyes in memory of those early starts. 'Young and stupid, playing cards till midnight and starting work around 2 am.' John had inherited all the personality of the family, outgoing and gregarious.

A year later on 22 November 1941, John and Grace tied the knot at the Baptist Church in Ballarat and moved permanently to the Melbourne suburb of Fitzroy. Norman who signed as one of the marriage certificate witnesses was soon to walk his own matrimonial path. This was to be the last occasion that the whole family was to celebrate together.

Two weeks later on 7 December 1941, Japan declares war on America after a first strike against the US fleet in Pearl Harbour on the island of Hawaii. The unprecedented attack now drew Great Britain and Australia into the Pacific War. Japan looked to expand its empire south seeking raw materials and land conquest. Australia was under threat. Australians who had not previously enlisted began to step forward and the second family loss was at hand.

In April 1942, George Edwin, now 68, fell ill and passed away, his death leaving a grieving family and heralding the passing of a generation.

H Evens & Sons, April 25, 1942. Funeral expenses of late George Edwin James died 23/4/42. Aged 68. Polished coffin. Hearse and 2 coaches.

Edna, now in her mid-thirties is the homemaker and full-time career for Mary as Norm enlists. With John in Melbourne, her only local support is George and Tous. Turning from personal tragedy four months later, Norm, aged 31, has enlisted and reported for training at Maribyrnong in Melbourne. He was posted to join 55 Composite Anti-Aircraft Regiment while John's attempts to enlist failed as he was categorised as medically unfit and returned to work at his trade.

Almost 12 months to the date of John's marriage, the last James boy completes his marriage vows. Norm and Gwen married in St Peter's Church in Ballarat with his brother John as the witness.

Whether best man for each other is unclear but their signature appears on each other's marriage certificate implying the strong bond between them. Sadly for the couple both male parents were deceased. Supposedly wartime honeymoons are brief and in Norm's case he was soon back on deployment. Humffray Street was now the domain of women, with his mother and sister its only occupants. Mary, now 66 and largely dependent on her daughter is now an onlooker to these events. With two more sister-in-laws to provide a wider range of conversations, Edna is delighted with her brothers' choices. Yet except for Tous, both Grace and Gwen are in Melbourne.

She has also moved into a new relationship after meeting an eligible widower at the Railway Institute Saturday dance. Nearly 80 years on, it is somewhat difficult to unpick the tapestry of that period.

Marriage and a new beginning

Joseph Denman was a mystery to his children and remained a mystery beyond his death in 1966. What brought my parents together is known only between them and has remained a secret beyond their death many years apart. Undoubtedly like all romances, it combines a little moonlight, some music and the beat of life's drums.

Their marriage in September 1943 was to culminate in bringing two families together, for each brought dependents from their past. Edna and Joe exchanged vows at the St Alipius Catholic Church in Ballarat, only blocks from Edna's former home in Stawell Street. Attending as witness is her long-time friend Clarice and husband Fred Sparkman.

The Certificate of Marriage notes their status as widower and spinster and that the groom has three living children. Edna had become a stepmother to three boys.

Certificate of Marriage: Register No. 560, 11 September 1943

Wedding day 1943

For someone bought up in the Methodist faith Edna's marriage in a Catholic church seems to draw little concern in the family, yet it was a time when there was much community division between the faiths and Ballarat had always had a strong Catholic base.

The Great Depression at the Door

At the time of their marriage, Joe is living at 319 Ligar Street, Ballarat North, a home bought earlier by his eldest sister and her husband. The property, originally an investment, was a four-bedroom Canadian style house with adequate space for his former wife and family.

319 Ligar Street, 2018

Ligar Street lays a couple of blocks east of Lydiard Street and is a short walk to the station. This thoroughfare is almost unchanged from earlier days except for the bitumen crown of the road surface. It is a wide open street with deep guttering between the road surface and the footpath. It implies by design that the winter season embraces the cold and occasional deluges.

Ligar Street South is predominately blue-collar working class with the odd professional and business family in its folds.

Many occupants of the street were to become neighbours and friends that were to share the next period of her life. Families such as the Speechleys, Oxbrows, the widow Anderson, Mrs Codey and Mrs Willis suggest Ballarat still retained their strong Anglo-Saxon roots. The years of large European immigration were still in the future. Edna was to join her husband in Ligar Street leaving her mother at Humffray Street. She has joined a wider family than just three boys who have been hived off to various relations since his former wife's untimely death.

Joe was the second eldest of four surviving children. He had an older sister Irene, now Mrs Andrew Bolger, a younger brother Harry (Henry) and younger sister Anne, living with his mother. Another sister had died as a child in Western Australia. Aged 14, Joseph Denman had joined the Victorian Railways to be trained as an under gear repairer. Initially he was transferred to Melbourne with stints at Newport and North Melbourne.

Five years later and he is in demand, moving around the State in various relieving positions, when the usual occupants were on holiday or long service leave, or during extended illness periods.

Every depot was different but always home in the comfort of the Railway Institute with its family embrace. Prior to his marriage to Eileen Martin he may have been seen as a rail vagabond moving from depot to depot.

Joe had been occupying Ligar Street alone since the death of his wife in late 1939.

Joe's family story

Joe's early life might well be categorised as rocky, with events in his childhood overcome with stoic determination. Born in Kalgoorlie-Boulder to parents of different faiths, father Church of England and mother Roman Catholic, his early life was entwined in the bustle of the Western Australian goldfields. His father had followed his older brother to the West, seeking his fortune. Within a year his mother had completed the journey where she married Thomas Henry in Fremantle in 1901. Tragically, a year later, Thomas' brother drowned in a tropical cyclone. A partner in a pearling business, he leaves his brother a generous benefactor. Life for this family now takes on a little prosperity as his father moves to Kalgoorlie-Boulder and undertakes some commercial ventures with various degrees of success, yet sadness continues to follow. Joseph by the age 10 is part of an expanding family, with an older sister, and two younger siblings. He understands loss with the death of a sibling of typhoid and then tragedy strikes again, when his father is killed in a mining accident.

Far from her roots, his mother has little option but to return to her hometown and family. Mary was born in Ballarat, so the Denman family is gathered up and commences their journey, first by rail, then ship, then rail again to their mother's city of birth. After a brief period of struggle, Mary made a heart-wrenching decision. Joe and Harry were left in custody of the Ballarat Orphanage while their mother undertook full-time work and the care of the two girls. This separation lasted some 13 months before the boys were reunited with the family. This period had been securely locked away and unknown until extensive research long after his death.

The man who was to be my father resided in Ballarat but possibly never settled. From the orphanage to various houses his life followed a pattern of change that included houses in Yuille Street, Lyons Street and then Ascot Street as the forerunners of later work depots. They became whistlestop homes.

In 1934 he married a girl from Snake Valley whom he met in the dining room at the Ballarat station. A year later and the first of their children are born. Another year on and a second boy is added as Eileen suffers the first signs of disease. Diagnosed with tuberculosis she is home isolated before being recommended to a sanatorium. Again pregnant with her newest child she survives childbirth before falling to this deadly disease. Francis my oldest half-brother was born in 1935, Brian in 1936 and Noel in 1938.

It could be contemplated that Edna's married life commenced with a few deep breaths and a spring clean. For latter generations who bask in today's comforts, in the mid-twentieth century, 319 Ligar Street was reflective of most local homes. It was built in the style of a Californian bungalow (circa 1910–1930) designed with four bedrooms, lounge, kitchen and separate bathroom; water, gas and electricity were connected. The kitchen stove was still wood burning and refrigeration out of range of the working wage. Ice was delivered in summer for the ice chest and winter's cold combatted by open fire hearths in every bedroom, including the main lounge room.

A gas heater utilised by a coin system enabled a bath to be filled with hot water. The toilet was outside under the pear tree.

No easy challenge for any woman regardless of the time and period. Second marriages and acceptance by another's children are not altogether unusual in any generation, but seen through the lens of time and recent conversations problematic and chancy.

New arrivals

Now in his mid-eighties, the eldest of Joe's three children my half-brother, Frank has little memory of his mother but identifies completely with his maternal grandparents who in all intents raised him. Living initially on a farm beyond Carngham and Snake Gully, he recognised his father from infrequent visits and saw his grandparents as parents and his direct family. After the death of his grandfather William

Martín, the family moved into Skipton Street, Ballarat. From this time his maternal grandmother raised him. Attempts to settle young Francis into Ligar Street was almost a bridge too far and at first was artfully resisted with youthful determination ... another early challenge. Of the other boys, Brian was living at Skipton with an aunt and Noel with his paternal grandmother, Mary Denman. Noel born just six months before Eileen's death knew no other family.

Weeks after Edna's marriage, she became an auntie for the first time, another role but with shared joy. Norm and Gwen James welcomed their first born, a son, Philip Edward James. A new generation is started. A year into Edna's marriage and she is pregnant, while her younger brother and wife announce their first addition, Peter. The James families were raining babies.

In late 1943, the war against the axis powers now begins its inevitable swing towards an Anglo/American victory. From 1942, American land and naval forces had begun to arrive in Australia. By mid-1943 some 150,000 troops were located in Queensland, mainly at Brisbane, Rockhampton and Townsville. Norm was part of that migration north. Only months after the bombing of Pearl Harbour, Darwin was attacked. In February 1942 and over the next 18 months Darwin and other Northern locations were regularly bombed. In November 1943, 55 Composite Anti-Aircraft Regiment departed Mt Isa by road arriving at Fenton airfield where they were initially deployed. Other locations included Fannie Bay.

The Great Depression at the Door

Darwin had become the most bombed city in Australia. Norm James's enlistment has seen him as part of that defending force, far away from his new son and loved ones.

Locals were experiencing a culture shock with American troops billeted in Ballarat between mid-1942 and 1943, many in private homes with the majority in a tent complex at Victoria Park. According to *The Courier* many expressed surprise on seeing the first American Negro GIs in uniform. Before war's end, many of these young men were to bleed out in many zones of the Pacific.

Dennis Joseph was born at the Ballarat Base Hospital on 4 September 1944.

Kitty Ellis & Dennis 1944

The allies had landed in Europe and within a year Germany had surrendered. Regrettably distant from home Norm was to learn of the death of his eldest brother. George had died on 21 May, two weeks after war's end in Europe casting a wreath of sadness over the surviving family. George's obituary in part heralds his passing.

Mr James was held in the highest of esteem by all who knew him, and the deepest sympathy is felt for the widow in her loss. The chief mourners were Mrs James (wife) Mrs James Sen. Mr & Mrs J Parkes, Mr & Mrs Denman, Mr & Mrs N James, Mr & Mrs J James, also numerous uncles, aunts, cousins and friends.

Among the family, his mother and sister lose their long-term ally and rock. George had died without any children and his wife Tous, never remarried.

> **15 August 1945: Japan unconditionally surrenders ending the Second World War.**

CHAPTER 4

Family Life and Motherhood

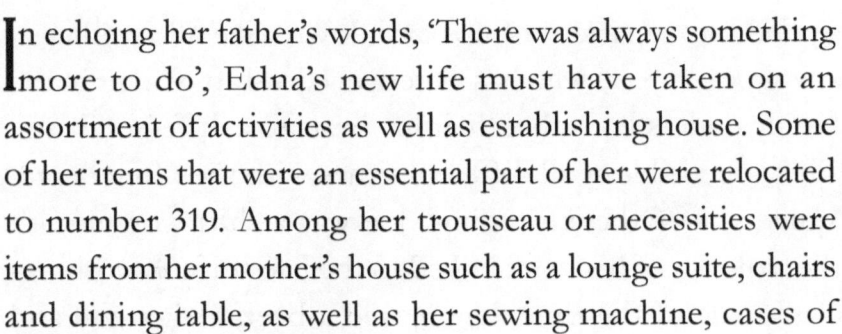

In echoing her father's words, 'There was always something more to do', Edna's new life must have taken on an assortment of activities as well as establishing house. Some of her items that were an essential part of her were relocated to number 319. Among her trousseau or necessities were items from her mother's house such as a lounge suite, chairs and dining table, as well as her sewing machine, cases of clothes, materials and goodies.

Although starting a new phase of life, she wasn't a novice homemaker and brought an array of skills and talents to the marriage. Adjustment and accommodation were surely a part of her initial months of marriage and bringing the children under one roof was part of this phase. At the time Joe's eldest son Frank was nine, and attending school in South Ballarat. Brian, aged seven, was living at Skipton and had been involved in an accident that was to leave him permanently scarred. Forever a mystery, a reputed fall as a toddler resulted in one leg being shorter by several inches. (13 cm). Successive operations of the period were unsuccessful and led him to wear a raised insert on his boot or shoe on the shortened leg.

This incident never restricted his movement but was to lead to many periods of months in and out of hospital in coming years. Noel Patrick Denman was nearing school age and had been in his grandmother's care since near birth.

This was the parcel accepted by Edna as she went about bringing order to 319 Ligar Street. One may expect that life settled into a pattern of ups and downs like all families at any time. Anyone who has experienced a shift worker in the family understands that their life beats to a different drum. They are visible at all different times with the often heard, 'quiet, your father's sleeping'. Joe was a shift worker with the majority of his work linked to the late shift. A working-class male of the time, he enjoyed a beer, a cigarette and the punt. Normal socialisation is limited, as weekends are included in the shift cycle.

At home he tends an expansive area at the house's rear with a thriving vegetable garden and hens kept for eggs and the occasional meal. Here the garden was a common love as both were the recipients of green thumbs. Joe maintained

Family Life and Motherhood

rich soil enriched with 'chook' poo and other additives. Edna enjoyed this mutual activity and added flowers and colour to the front and back gardens. Scents and colour could be bought from outside to the table setting. Her favourites included Lily of the Valley, freesias, and pink hydrangeas. Still, seasons came and went and birthdays celebrated the next phase and progress of individuals. Bicycles were the most sought after present and everyone enjoyed the ride to freedom. Frank was forever at his grandmother's and with the other boys within the local street orbit. Dennis clearly remembers his reconditioned and brightly painted red bike that enabled frequent trips to his Uncle Harry and Auntie Edna's home. It was a city of relative safety with an abundance of mothers' eyes constantly on children at play. Yet there were occasional day-to-day dramas and a few memories that Mum can readily recall.

Imagine today this event. Standing on the footpath outside the house she turned to a lusty SHOUT. 'Clear the fence madam!' As she turned, she was met with a group of wild-eyed steers galloping down the street. With an immediate response, she lifted a small boy and herself over the height of the front fence to gaze at the threat thundering by.

'Good job Mrs,' was the call, as the horseman rode in their wake.

Beyond the daily routine, holidays at Geelong and day rail trips were part of the family lifestyle as railway workers were eligible for free travel passes during these periods. No journey on a steam train was to be bettered without a car in the family.

The train journey to Spencer Street Station was a special event to visit Joe's sister Irene and her children. They had moved to the city after the death of her husband. Irene had settled in Canterbury in a delightful period home with stained glass windows near the station. A fleeting memory is still retained of Edna's son as they enjoyed a different world and greater comforts of home. Irene was another sister-in-law who on the Denman side clearly enjoyed her company. Edna even managed a 'girls' weekend with Kitty and child to enjoy a short break in the 'Big Smoke', but that was a rarity. Steam locomotives had been the predominant motive power for the state's many country services. The usual passenger train consisted of an R class passenger engine and first and second class carriages. Dennis can remember a number of trips where an open window was a magnet for small boys to extend their view. Naturally against all advice a spec of soot or containment soon resulted in red stinging eyes and a few tears. A mother's role is never done. Steam was on the decline and memories of being lifted into the cab of the first electric diesel locomotive that sat in Ballarat Station are still vivid. Outside his parents looked on from the crowded platform.

Other events were also part of the times where occupational holidays and picnics were held by many local union or business groups, such as the butchers' picnic, the firemen's picnic and so on. These were times of shared family fun and games. The railways had their day of entertainment and for wives a day without housework. Edna and Joe were visible participants.

Making connections

Number 319 was a house that buzzed to the noise of children as they spilled from the length of the street. Edna's son was part of a cadre of similar aged boys as his older brothers took to their own age groups. Playmates from the immediate circle were the two boys of the Dunn family, Peter Bergen, Denis Bolster and Johnny Allen, all within the street. For Edna, family and friends balanced her life as she maintained her strong connections to her brothers and their families.

Walking the walk – Sturt Street

From single and childless, she advanced in a relatively short time to mother and stepmother. In addition, her role as aunt expanded to more James children. John and Grace added another son, Barry, and later a daughter named Gloria was to swell John James' family. Norm and Gwen have a second son, Trevor Maxwell to complete their brood. On the Denman side, Joe's eldest sister Irene has a son, Michael and daughter, Margaret. Anne has two boys, Norman and Kevin Rowe.

Family Life and Motherhood

The two sisters are different in looks and personality and live different lives based on income. Andrew Bolger is from a successful grazier's family and from this income enabled Rowen & Co. investment opportunities, including 319 Ligar Street.

Edna's neighbours quickly recognised her qualities and the size of the task, possibly with a degree of sympathy. They readily respond to her open personality and warmth. Word of mouth would soon circulate the arrival of a busy wife and skilled dressmaker. The Singer sewing machine had a new home.

Read before operating

To the ears of a child the sound comes in spurts with irregular short stops. It is a sort of chatter that comes as the needle rises and falls. Not unlike the chatter of little capuchin monkeys that sees the movement of a predator sliding through the trees. The needle stroke is rapid as it plunges the thread through the material. The skilled operative uses both hands to guide the material squarely to the thread as the foot initiates the peddle drive. Within a short period Edna had a circle of customers that helped supplement her husband's wage and led to the deposit to buy the house from her sister-in law.

It was a busy time and years passed quickly. Somewhere in this later period Edna's mother arrived, which required a reorganising of the living arrangements. Forever lost the reason of her mother's arrival, but illness and repeated periods of depression is the likely cornerstone that saw Mary united with her daughter. The loss of her husband and oldest son had bought on periods of despair which led to her being unable to cope alone.

The first strains of my parents' relationship were near at hand. This is obviously conjecture but within a year or two major changes occurred.

Family Life and Motherhood

Busy days

In 1950, the Australian community were again pulled towards another war. The Korean War commenced in the middle of the year when the communist north invaded the democratic south. The peninsula had been partitioned in 1945 between zones of influence, North and South. This faraway conflict was to have little or no impact on the families in Ligar Street but another event that year did. An ongoing pay dispute between the rail unions and the Victorian Government irreversibly stalled. From October to December 1950, Victorian members of the Australian Railway Unions (ARU) and the Australian Federated Union of Locomotive Enginemen (AFULE) stopped work.

This was to be the longest railway strike in Victorian history and overnight placed Edna's husband without an income. The Ballarat railyard and all train operations ceased. Without work, the Railway Institute became the respite for the rail community as meetings and social activities filled the days. At hand the North Star Hotel sat adjacent the Institute.

Overnight it may have seemed that the lights were turned off, yet like the privations of the Depression years this woman held firm and made the best of the circumstances. Yet tensions must have continued to peck at the marriage. Unknown or shared are any periods of grief or the odd tear. Still close friends, family and neighbours continued to provide support with acts of kindness. Johnny and family for a Sunday lunch with an armful of goodies and supplies. With an open door policy, all were welcome and freshly baked scones always at hand. To little kids around the age of her sons, the best cordial and cupcakes or chocolate crackles were always on offer at Mrs Denman's. I can still taste the chocolate icing scraped from the bowl with a wooden spoon as a young boy. Such were the delights of being in the kitchen when my mother was baking.

Next door, an elderly Mrs Willis was always good for a few hours of childminding. On the other side were Keith and Margaret Allen. Keith was one of three brothers who operated and ran Allen's Jewellers. Neighbours of a difference whose properties shared a common wall – Keith in a white shirt and suit who daily drove to work and my father in his overalls and hat cycling to and from the railway shunting yard.

Edna's new life was busy, yet the loss of her brother George as confidante and sounding board can't be understated.

The year 1952 sees the three older boys attending Catholic schools. The Martins and Gran Denman are practising Catholics and probably made the decision for the boys' education. Joseph, though married and bought up in the Catholic faith, is seemingly distant from these decisions and religion takes little or no part of his life. Dennis has commenced school at the Macarthur Street State and Frank will soon begin work at the Myer Mill.

Family Life and Motherhood

This year is additionally a busy time for her sewing machine, as she notes in a little red-covered book. Clearly personal and forgotten, the book was found long after her death. Her script is clear as she records the work and payment.

Mrs White, dress: 1 pound 10 shillings
Mrs Dunn, overcoat: 4 pound 10 shillings
Mrs Marsh, summer coat: 1 pound 5 shillings
Ada Pinny, pants: 15 shillings
Mrs Gibson, blazer: 2 pound

The list continues for many more lines but clearly identifies a busy life that compliments home care. This record continues for another year with entries of more work and an insight into the monetary stress at number 319.

Mrs Rankin, skirt & jacket: 1 pound 2 shillings & 6 pence
Mrs Wright, 2 pleated skirts: 1 pound 5 shillings
Mrs Glover, blazer & dress: 3 pound 10 shillings
Betty, shirt and shorten skirt: 13 shillings
Mrs Gordon, skirt: 12 shillings & sixpence
Mrs Davey, sun suit: 1 pound 5 shilling

Read today it resembles an account ledger and continues the costs of family presents for birthdays and the like. So much generosity for others before thoughts of self continues to unfold. The list is long and varied for family and friends; small examples indicate family first. Singlets and underpants for Frank, runners for Noel, socks and shorts for Brian, coloured pencils and a book for Dennis, Johnnie's family, Norm's family, present for mum ...

> **Australia moved to decimal currency in 1966. 1 pound converted to 2 dollars, 1 pound = 20 shillings, 10 shillings converted to 1 dollar and 1 shilling = 12 pence or 10 cents.**

Much is going on in Edna's life as she glides through the years of middle age and the number 50 looms.

Sturt Street Ballarat 1949

Household work is not very different from the earlier generation, cooking is still undertaken by wood heated stoves, with gas and electric stoves not in every household. Washing machines and refrigerators are in higher income families (but not in 319) and the radio the main source of news and entertainment. Radio plays and music registered by huge audiences, with favourites rating for years. Evenings may combine knitting jumpers for the boys or her husband and darning socks to close a normal day. Cards games were very much a family entertainment, whether lone in patience or partnering in crib or euchre. Shades of 1950s domesticity; and somewhere in that year a major disruption or event occurs that leads to Edna's mother moving out and relocating to Melbourne.

This period was never spoken of and never shared except in the general way of separation by both parents in later years.

> **The first Begonia Festival commences Saturday 8 March 1953.**

Separation

Sadly some insight may be suggested by the affidavit presented to the Supreme Court of Victoria (1967) many years later.

Between the said marriage date and about the year 1952 the said deceased gave me housekeeping money which was sufficient in view of his earnings. The said deceased was a heavy drinker and keen gambler and used his own money for these things but later reduced this figure to 10 shillings per week. I took in dressmaking and alterations to supplement this loss and run the house.

Sometime towards the end of 1953 my parents separated. In truth I have no memory of this period but again an extract from the earlier affidavit implies possibly why:

As I had received little money from him for two years and he was telling me to leave, I consulted a solicitor in Ballarat in respect to my financial position and also because it was becoming unbearable to continue living with the deceased.

CHAPTER 5

A New Start in Melbourne

We arrived in Melbourne towards the Christmas holidays and for a brief period stayed with Norm and Gwen. How the contents of 10 years of marriage came to Melbourne is unknown, but we were soon united with her mother in the suburb of Kew. Set in the leafy folds beyond Studley Park and the Yarra River, it is relatively prosperous, with wealth visible in the riverside homes and surrounds to lesser income level in East Kew.

Kew was to replace Ballarat as home for the rest of her life. It was to provide many happy memories and new chapters of friendships and of course, continuous hard work; yet they were steps in her future and much was to occur on the way.

Marvellous Melbourne, the Victorian capital, had spread to all points of the compass with continuous suburban sprawl. The wealthier suburbs clung to shores of Port Phillip Bay and reached to the shade of the Dandenongs. With a series of magnificent inner city parks or green spaces complimenting its commercial city, Melbourne was the engine room of the State's economy with the 'golden mile' of commerce and retail shopping at its centre. Public transport radiated from its heart with both electric trams and train services timetabled to enable reasonable destinations access to the city. Less desirable suburbs or working class families were nearer to industry and lay to the north and west.

Edna's choice of living arrangements were somewhat determined by her extended family. Always a central part of her life, she had remained in close contact throughout those many years. Although most of the previous generation had passed on, a strong link had been maintained by their offspring. Over those years, life events had been shared between the family members and acknowledged with cards and birth gifts. Among this generation were the offspring of John Alfred's children and one of these cousins lived in Kew. Ernest Hector, still a bachelor, lived at 122 Peel Street with his single brother Hilton. Sprinkled around other suburbs were other siblings including George Desmond, Florence Helena and the youngest, Lillian Kathleen. John Stanley (letter writer to 10-year-old Edna) was living in Sydney.

A New Start in Melbourne

Fortunately or of necessity there was room for Edna and one small boy who were warmly welcomed into Peel Street. This was the sanctuary that Edna's mother had found her way to months before. This was to be our residential address for the next couple of years.

Initially the 'Things to do' list must have been daunting – the endless minutiae of government and officialdom. In order of importance were income and a school for her son's continued education. Again through an extended relative contact, Edna was introduced to a tailoring business and a man who was to assist her in future years. This person was Ray Lilford of Lilford Bros, tailors of high-end quality men's and women's suits and garments. Ray Lilford can readily be recalled to her son's eyes 60 years on. An excessively tall man, aged in his late 50s with sparkling eyes behind horn-rimmed glasses. Softly spoken he was exquisitely dressed in light grey suit pants with a silver waistcoat over a lightly striped, white shirt.

Around his neck was the classic tailor's tape and he carried his marking chalk in his waistcoat pocket.

Edna commenced a trial period with Lilford's soon after her interview and in February of 1954, Dennis commenced school at Kew State.

> **First Royal visit to Australia of a reigning monarch occurred in March 1954, Queen Elizabeth II and her consort Prince Philip the Duke of Edinburgh.**

The Royal Visit in 1954 continued the English-Australian monarchal system and propelled school age children to be bussed to locations to wave a cheery welcome. The students of 1075, Kew State Primary School were part of this throng.

Once more the rhythm of work, rest and more work consumed Edna's life. Lilford Bros shop was located near the Kew Junction and was either a five-minute bus ride or 20-minute walk.

Edna's finances dictated that most times she walked. Walking twice daily showed once more a steely determination to move forward. Near at hand was the local shopping centre of the North Kew Village in Willsmere Road and the local dairy. Here locals arrived daily to buy a 'billy' full of milk for a shilling. Also within this precinct was the local Methodist church in Pakington Street. Whether as a sup to her mother or a need of comfort it's possible that Edna sensed the need of some stability beyond her capacity to provide. This little church was to play a part in widening a circle of friends and provide her son with the grounding of faith. A highly unsuccessful pursuit on the part of her son but allowed an insight into community and friendship. Here was an opportunity for Edna to sing psalms and songs of praise in community and where she met the Stormonth family,

A New Start in Melbourne

Lena and her maiden sister Ettie Barnard.

Lena was the mother of two children, Lorraine, a year older than Dennis and John a year younger. They were to become great playmates and the women long-term friends. Kew was providing the first steps of stability in many a year.

> **The first Moomba parade in 1954.**

Not every day's events or experiences will ever be remembered, or if they are, remembered with any accuracy. Two years passed quickly and in greater Melbourne the 1956 Olympic Summer Games were the headline act. Between 10 June and 8 December the city welcomed the world. Twelve days after her son's 12th birthday, Australia's first television broadcast occurred in Sydney. Along with her son the nearest she got to program viewing was from the pavement outside an electrical retail shop. For the consumer, it was marketing at its best.

Connections new and old

With all the wider family now resident in Melbourne, visits between the brothers and sister were organised loosely on a monthly turn. This gave Mary an opportunity to see both her other children and grandchildren.

The James Families (John, Grace, Mary, Gwen & Norm)

Norm after being discharged from the army had returned to the trade and commenced work with Pettigrews. In 1948 his family had moved to Ashburton when commission homes were made available to returned service personnel. John after years of double shifts had quickly moved from employee to self-employed and purchased a shopfront and residence in the western suburb of Seddon.

In Power Street, Kew a certain rhythm and pattern settled in as Lilford's business continued to expand and Edna was offered overtime on Saturday mornings. Clearly a more than competent tailoress she mixes well with the other women and with the boss. The extra money was surely needed but left little time to watch over the comings and

A New Start in Melbourne

goings of her 12-year-old child. Fortunately, he was blessed with schoolboy friends whose parents were able to part adopt him as he visited with their children. As can occur, the connection between grandson and grandmother was tenuous and with growing independence his preference was other environments.

One such family was Ivor and Joyce Lloyd who sons, John and older brother James were a successful part of his growth. Within this household he was ushered into their interests and pursuits. It was here that he learned snooker on the family table and crib, Ivor's favourite. His interests soared in a wider world from classical music to learning chess. Ivor and his brother were specialised small goods and food retailers with shops in Richmond and the City Market with much to interest a small boy. Additionally, Dennis had found a bolthole and regularly spent many after school hours at the local library.

A year on and Edna is soon to celebrate her 50th birthday. Her mother has turned 80 and though a little infirm is still independent. Edna's brothers support her in small ways with John always adding something extra. Never forgotten 10 pound notes surreptitiously placed with the cake offerings. Still after some years of consolidation the cousin has suggested it is time to move on. Reputedly Hector in late middle age has found a companion and wishes to consummate the relationship with her role as a housekeeper. Once again the caravan was on the move and relocated to a property a mere two streets away and closer towards the junction.

Brougham Street, Kew

Call it luck or random timing, but a widower client of Ray Lilford is looking for a housekeeper and agrees to house the trio. Alfred J Wynde is a city-based jeweller nearing retirement and Edna takes on the dual roles of housekeeper and cook as well as continuing her work at Lilfords. The rhetoric of a future Prime Minister was yet to be unleashed on the Australian public, *'Life wasn't meant to be easy'*.

Again the James family rallied and relocated all to their new address. Schooling for Dennis was unchanged as his time at Kew State was nearing completion. Number 60 Brougham Street was a solid and comfortable home where Edna shared a bedroom with her mother and Dennis was comfortably set up in an enclosed sleep-out on the rear verandah. Once more the theory of random events bought another family into Edna's life. Pop and Eve Hodgson were our new neighbours directly opposite and the link was almost instantaneous and for the term of their long lives. The Hodgson's additionally had three adult children, Jack the eldest and mostly absent on contract for the mining industry. Their other son Alan, in his mid-30s was on an invalid pension who took to the boy and a daughter, Beverly aged 19. For Edna and her young son this was

A New Start in Melbourne

an unlikely collection of people to become friends, yet a welcomed gift.

In future weeks Edna and her son were to consolidate their knowledge of the main Kew shopping strip and surrounds. In High Street at the junction of Brougham Street, 141 was the Newsagent, followed by the Radio Doctor, Progress Shoes, Singer's Fruiter, Adam's cake shop, the Grey Hound Hotel and then GJ Coles and Co. All soon within reach of a small boy who within the year started delivery papers for the newsagent. During this year another move was at hand.

After two decades in Denmark Street the brothers Lilford relocated away from the Junction. They moved to 214 High Street, Kew next to the Rialto theatre. It was at that site that Edna's son was to meet this kindly benefactor and gain an insight into his mother's work. Welcomed after school for brief periods, the construct of handmade suits unfolded as the 'boss' explained the sequence of material selection to measuring and the steps to make the finished item.

Slender and tall for his age, this dark-haired boy combined both genes of his parents with the John James height to follow. Alert and inquisitive, his manner and looks made acceptance by both his peer group and adults an open door for many households.

Edna has rapidly settled into this next life phase at Brougham Street. Mr Wynde, a small-framed man, makes little demands on the trio beyond his hot dinner and sweets. He spends his weekends in his garden and occasionally makes the trip to Glenferrie Oval as he is an avid Hawthorn Football Club supporter.

This year Edna turns 50 and celebrates with family at Ashburton. As may be expected the slender girlish figure has been replaced with a heavier frame and grey flecks intrude in her hair. She now requires reading glasses and walks a little slower. If she had time for the thought, she may have noted that the aging process is shared by all. Still unassuming and determined, she works tirelessly to keep her charges together and secure.

Ashburton is not so far as the crow flies but a route march for Edna and her son. This suburban journey commenced with the tram along Whitehorse Road to the Bourke Street terminus, another tram to Camberwell Station and then the shuttle train between Camberwell to Alamein Station. Throw in the blocks in-between and your fitness test is complete. The return in Norm's car was highly appreciated.

Gwen and Edna with sons about the same age are able to meet monthly in the city and often lunch in the Coles cafeteria. The cousins get on well and maintain a relationship long beyond childhood. At Seddon, her brother John and Grace have been slowly building their business. Working long hours, Edna's sister-in-law combined housekeeping with running the shop as John expands his reach to factories and new locations. John has additionally joined the Footscray Cricket Club and begins his affiliation with VFL football. If Edna is to be part of the football conversation, she too adopts Footscray. Grace who is slightly older than her husband is beginning to show the strains of their business life. John's occupation sees him starting work at three or four in the morning to fill orders and cake runs for two shops. To provide a little relief, Edna and Ettie Barnard take Dennis and Peter to Geelong for a brief five-day holiday.

Once again the relationship between sister and brother is quietly at hand. A memory another nephew will remember of his aunt long into adulthood.

Years follow and subtle changes are occurring. Joe has asked for access to his son and they meet monthly or irregularly in the city. The boy partitions his parents' lives and is comfortable in each company and connects with his brothers. Other than his uncles and before reconciled with his father the only males in his orbit were Hector and Mr Wynde. Dennis doesn't connect with either man and with nothing in common is polite and yet distant. As Eve Hodgson and Edna socialise, she is told about her daughter's suitor. Chas (Charles) Cornell a recent Korean veteran is soon to be a constructive role model for her son. As Chas builds his marriage house in Balwyn he acquires a readymade apprentice. Edna is silently delighted that her son has found a positive influence as he shadows the older man.

Change is brewing

The following years see the beginning of the change between mother and son. It is but the normal cycle of life, as one grows towards a teenager, the other moves through middle age to her next phase. This relocation has also meant Edna adopting a nearer church of her faith and a new congregation waits in Walpole Street.

Whether it reminded her of her childhood church will never be known but it provided a social content for the youth as well as church members, with weekend tennis and other activities. It was within this church that she commenced the steps of charity work and joined the Eye and Ear auxiliary.

Dennis has moved on to secondary education and started at Swinburne Technical College in Glenferrie. Here his mother continues her support by making a blazer to compliment the school uniform. Regardless of their social status the boy would continue to be presentable with jackets and suits all made at Lilfords and at the best rate in town. During this next period Edna found herself drawn into the lives of her new-found friends having introduced Eve to Ettie Barnard and Lena. Over scones and tea, they probably discussed the trivia of life and families, and on many an occasion, alterations or the colour of a new coat. The Singer was never idle.

When 1960 arrived, the trio were still entrenched at 60 Brougham Street, with Dennis's education nearing completion. She looks on at a youth who is heading towards six foot (181 cm) and will commence an apprenticeship in the following year. His scholastic results have been slightly above average but never outstanding. His personality with his peers has seen him selected as a prefect and may indicate an insight into his other abilities. He remains slender in build and is quietly spoken and opens up mainly in his select company. Mary, now in her eighties, continues to knit and crochet an endless array of items for charity, such as the Smith Family and the Red Cross.

> **Alfred J Wynde is to retire and sell the property to live with his son.**

Once more Edna is to be provided with a challenge that understandably may have brought moments of despair. Within the month, a solution is at hand and a little house is found. Whatever the backstory to the purchase it stayed in the realms of adults. Undoubtedly she consulted her brothers and particularly Johnnie, but with the approval of the bank and a term guarantee by Ray Lilford, the next move fell into place.

When things go wrong as they sometimes will,
When the road you're trudging seems all uphill,
When the funds are low and the debts are high,
and you want to smile but you have to sigh,
When care is pressing you down a bit –
rest if you must, but don't you quit.
Don't Quit, Edgar A Guest

CHAPTER 6

A Home of Her Own

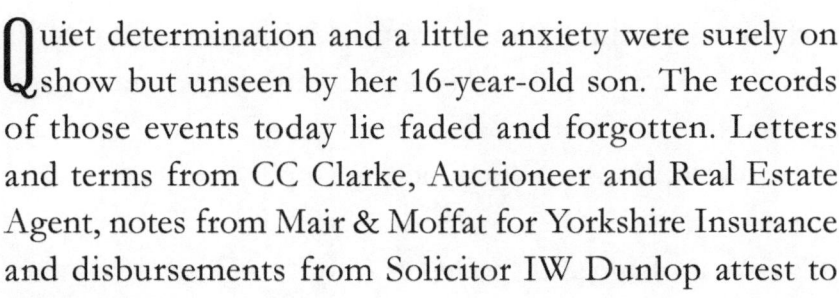

Quiet determination and a little anxiety were surely on show but unseen by her 16-year-old son. The records of those events today lie faded and forgotten. Letters and terms from CC Clarke, Auctioneer and Real Estate Agent, notes from Mair & Moffat for Yorkshire Insurance and disbursements from Solicitor IW Dunlop attest to commitment.

Their new home, 141 Brougham Street, is part of five properties that resemble the tenement homes of the English worker from an earlier century.

Hidden behind the brick Victorian façade this small home comprises two bedrooms, a sitting room, kitchen and bathroom. Room for all, as a shared bedroom is the lot of my mother, with the back bedroom set aside for her son.

Initially, even for a small house it lacked some furniture, but with the help of her brother and some savings, the additions to the house appeared. Comfortable chairs, a small glass-fronted cabinet and a new refrigerator.

Finally, from storage and boxes, Edna's prized dinner settings, crystal glasses and oddments could share her life.

Was there ever a day of rest might have briefly entered my mother's thoughts, but finally; a house to make a HOME of her own. Dennis is now employed as an electrical trade apprentice for the Victorian Railways. His journey starts early to catch the 6.25 am tram which makes the city in time for a 7.20 start. Quickly learned are the timetables for the no. 48 from North Balwyn and the 42 from Deepdene as regular options via the junction stop.

Regardless of age and spoiled as only a single child can be, Edna would be up early to cut or prepare his lunch before restarting her day and walking off to work. Her dress code for work was one of practicality. Blouse and skirt, either pleated or plain, dark blue or slate with a light jacket in summer. Twin sets were another standby and always comfortable walking shoes.

A Home of Her Own

With another wage incoming a moment of relief may have been observed but there was always something more to do. The work at home was still reflective of the many past years. This Victorian house contained gas for heating and cooking and a kitchen where the full suite of mains, soups and sweets could be prepared. Within this little kitchen she could turn her hand to long practised staples as well as receipts recorded over many years. Her recipe book, now aged and faded, lists both culinary delights and where they came from.

Among the sweets are a small sample of people who shared her life, including Gwen James (lemon biscuits), Lorna Davis (chocolate slice), Faye Osborne (boiled fruit cake), Ada Pinney (peppermint slice), Shirley Manns (plum pudding) and more.

Disappointedly, for washing clothes a copper was on hand with a mangle fixed to the wash troves. An everyday chore, cleaning clothes and bedsheets were long listed among a women's lot. Sort of sight unseen by her son but ever appreciated. A washing machine was years away.

Life proceeded to these roles as Edna continued work and elder care. Fortunately, with both working, a near neighbour has indicated she can keep an eye on Mary. Mrs Vallese or the 'Italian lady' as my mother continued to call her became another friend along with her daughter Rose. Her son came and went as he continued night school and different work locations and an outgoing social life. During this period Mary had a few medical turns and became reclusive in her bedroom chair.

Around this time television became part of the furniture. To Edna's surprise and delight her youngest brother arrived with a TV set. In John's eyes a small gift and a deep understanding of her journey, I suspect it was also an acknowledgement of the care provided for their mother.

The small screen had progressively revolutionised the community's home entertainment and now graced the trio with a variety of programs, from *Sunny Side-Up* to *In Melbourne Tonight*. Prior to this, the wider silver screen had long been a favourite of both mother and son.

With Lilford's next to the theatre, Edna soon became friends with the usher and staff and the odd free ticket came her way. Saturday matinees had been a staple part of her son's early years and together they had shared the occasional Friday evening screening. *The Robe* and *The King and I* were mainstream pictures but *Hopalong Cassidy* and cartoons were popcorn matinees. The theatre on a Saturday afternoon was the meeting place of many of Kew's attendee population.

A sad goodbye

Approaching her late 80s, Mary's health had slowly deteriorated, and in May of 1963 she passed away. Mary passing severed Edna's last link to her parents' generation and a pall of black hung over the house. Fortified with her brothers' assistance and sister-in-laws' support, a different future was to unfold.

Mary Elizabeth James had endured much in her lifetime and outlived her husband by some 20 years. She had qualities that wouldn't be seen by a younger generation and in her daughter's words had provided her children with a loving and happy family. She had been an accomplished amateur painter and played the piano in her pre-marriage years; aptitudes never on show as age and circumstances passed by.

Mary had seen many things and technological changes in her life, yet remained a woman of the Victorian age.

> **Mary joined her husband George in Ballarat's cemetery. New section 8, row 1, grave 37.**

Mary's death was the first in the wider family and the first exposure of this group of young people who called her 'Nana'. The older boys, Edna's nephews and son were nearing their 20s and the others in either their late or mid-teens. The experience and emotion of loss was apparent to all as we looked on at our parents. Words and expressions of comfort surrounded them as they congregated together. Edna is in her 56th year and in a strange way the loss of a loved one has opened the door to a degree of freedom. Her son has opted to spend almost every other weekend with his father and the city of her birth becomes an occasional dining table topic. Months on and Edna has the house to herself and widens her own social calendar. Dennis is progressing through his apprenticeship and his social life taken with ballroom dancing. Ray Barclay has asked him to be a groomsman at his wedding; it is to be the first of many.

Methodist Church Kew 1963

A Home of Her Own

The next generation grows

The rite of passage of 21 and majority is first celebrated by Edna's eldest nephew, Phillip James in September 1964. Two very proud parents and wider family join together for a do. This coming of age and the right to vote is followed the next year by Peter in January, then Dennis in September. For the weekend of early September 1965, the little house in Brougham Street surged to the sound of voices and clink of glasses. The welcoming hostess in the guise of my mother has once again provided finger food and options a plenty.

Edna in many ways has been adopted by her son's friends, all part of the Dance Court fraternity. They are well known to the woman of the house and in preceding years had like seagulls consumed her coffee and snacks. They called her Mrs D as she happily embraced this new generation of both girls and young men. Without a car, most had become her son's transporters for functions near and far.

The social life at Dance Court was the predominant link in her son's life, as he partnered debutants and progressed in medal dancing. From dress suits to tails she was continuously involved in support of his activities. From within this happy period another dark cloud appeared as John's wife passed away. Ethel Grace James was not to reach old age or regrettably live to see her children grow or hug a grandchild.

Grace passed away aged 52, leaving three children and a distraught husband. Once more the family came together to farewell a much loved woman. Beyond the loss the reality of life continues. Unasked and never forgotten between brother and sister were the Saturday tram and train rides to Seddon station and then more blocks before arriving at Charles Street. Not bad for 'an old girl' nearing her 60th year. Even so she had experienced a shortening of breath in the earlier months and was under doctor's orders 'to slow down'. Yet to her nephews and niece, Edna wasn't a replacement mum, just their aunt who on a weekly basis was to wash clothes and organise the housework. If she was able to assist her niece or nephews in their loss is today unknown; but for her brother, it was a god sent.

News from Ballarat

A day after her son's most recent return from Ballarat there was a late night knock on the door. Edna was confronted with Brian Denman who passed on the news of Dennis' father's death.

Early in April 1966, Joseph Denman suffered a massive heart attack and died alone aged 60. Noel had returned from his workday to find his father prone on the kitchen floor. Twelve odd years after their separation and with minimal contact between them, her son's father was deceased. In earlier years, Dennis had been the go-between with child support but that had ceased at 16 years of age.

His funeral took place in Ballarat with arrangements made by his sister Anne and husband Norm Rowe to be buried in the Martin family plot at Carngham. Dennis joined Brian and Noel in mourning with Frank absent residing in London.

Extract of Death no. 8330/66. 27th April 1966
Joseph Denman, Railway employee, Male 60 years. Address: 319 Ligar Street, Ballarat.

Alas for the Denman boys the loss of a parent was still somewhat raw when their Uncle Harry died suddenly. Harry (Henry) Denman was a year younger than his brother. He was a quiet, unassuming individual and left his wife Edna, another widow with the surname of Denman. Although distant, the thoughts of one widow to another could only be expressed by a card and words of condolences. The sister-in-laws had maintained their link throughout the separation. Again the cycle of life with all its mysteries left the survivors to pick up the pieces and move forward.

Somehow attempting to balance this year of sorrow, events now quietly turned to bring some joy into the little home. Her son's contemporaries who had visited and socialised at her table now introduced partners and fiancées. Weddings were on the menu and Dennis was to play a secondary part in many of them. His commitment was still distant.

Ray & Joan Sevior, 1967

Graeme & Raeleen Besnard, Virginia, South Australia

A Home of Her Own

First artificial satellite to orbit the moon.

Edna was to watch on as her son was swept along with his friends' weddings. A near neighbour's son, Ian Le Page, surprisingly asked Dennis to be his groomsman. A month later and he joins another wedding party for Roger Gough and Julie, followed by best man for Don and Elizabeth Shell. Diamonds appeared on small left hands as proposals were accepted as another of her son's close friends planned their weddings. Ray Sevior has been particularly close to Edna and commenced the next wedding round with the invitation to Dennis and Mrs D (not partner). Ray's future wife Joan surprisingly shares the same surname of Denman (no relation). It is soon to change. Edna was to attend the church and festivity and watch her son as best man and his engaging social skills. It was here that mother and son graced the floor together and confirmed her long silent skills, a foxtrot and a gentle waltz … not bad for an old girl.

The entrance to the house became a revolving door as her son's social activities increased. He has been long involved with Gwenda whom he met at Dance Court, but is continuously distracted by his lifestyle. He has completed a supervisory certificate at RMIT, since qualifying as a tradesman and is now working Saturday mornings and occasionally all weekend. She understands from her own journey that additional income means security or options. The new year brings his first large investment with the purchase of a car. Once more a vanishing sight as with independent wheels his range grows. Along the way, mother and son combine to buy a new lounge setting and comfortable chairs. Edna has continued to work through all of the events of the preceding years and recently faced a new employer. After many long years Lilford Bros has ceased and A & O Dour takes over the business. Again blessed with an engaging employer she acknowledges the demand of hand sewing is wearing her out. Edna at 60 has reached retirement age, but continues to work for another few years.

CHAPTER 7

Ups and Downs and Roundabouts

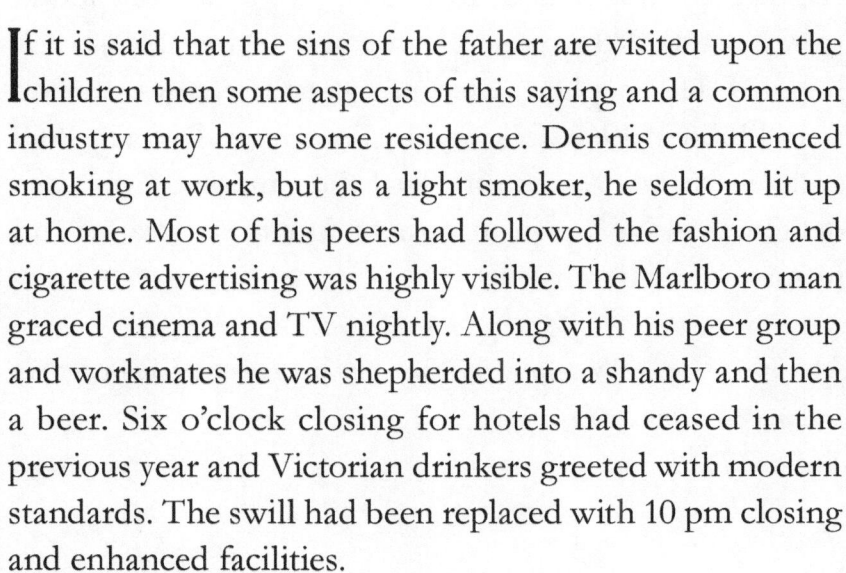

If it is said that the sins of the father are visited upon the children then some aspects of this saying and a common industry may have some residence. Dennis commenced smoking at work, but as a light smoker, he seldom lit up at home. Most of his peers had followed the fashion and cigarette advertising was highly visible. The Marlboro man graced cinema and TV nightly. Along with his peer group and workmates he was shepherded into a shandy and then a beer. Six o'clock closing for hotels had ceased in the previous year and Victorian drinkers greeted with modern standards. The swill had been replaced with 10 pm closing and enhanced facilities.

Events once planned around train timetables could now occur at a whim. The independence of wheels was a boon to both mother and son. The call of long missed friends and acquaintances was only a two-hour drive. Norm and Ada Pinney can now enjoy a hug and embrace, instead of a letter or postcard. The Pinny's have three children and the youngest is to play a large part in Edna's later years. Within the year Edna is deposited in Ballarat for a reunion of her friends Clarice and Kitty. Reputedly the conversation went long into the night and the following day.

Mrs S Stormonth requests the pleasure of your company at the marriage of her daughter Lorraine Ethel to ... at St John's Church, Toorak.

This younger generation were addicted to marriage.

All through this period, Edna's nephews had also found mates. Auntie Edna was to have a seat at the table as each married. Her nephews were to take their vows year on year, Philip in 1968, followed by Peter, then Barry in 1969 and Trevor in 1971 commenced their unions. Edna was delighted to be drawn into these functions as aunt and unspoken matriarch.

Mrs E Denman, we thank you for your company and lovely gift on this our wedding day.
Val and Philip

Dear Auntie Edna, we wish to thank you most sincerely for the lovely gift and kind wishes on the occasion of our wedding.
Jan & Barry
(All keepsakes and memories)

Beyond her family, Edna finds herself carried along with another of her son's cadre and is Adelaide-bound. William and Violet Battersby were pleased to announce the wedding of their eldest son Ian to Carol Fenton. As Dennis is in the wedding party the Battersbys provide a chauffeur service and accommodation for Edna to Adelaide. The following year and Graeme Besnard marries a former Miss Virginia from the South Australian State and once more Edna attends as her son joins the wedding party. Commencing married life back in Melbourne, Raelene is another who warmly embraces Edna.

Retirement

Naturally along with these happy times there are many solitary moments as she continues her journey. Towards the end of the decade, her working life ceases for retirement. There is little celebration to this event that passes quietly at week's end. Edna adjusts to a different lifestyle with quieter spells as the conversation of the workplace recedes and like the seasons follows in its stead. Ground to be turned, weeds to pull and rich loam topped up for tomatoes and always her beautiful hydrangeas to attend. The garden is her place of contentment. Images can be readily formed of my mother kneeling on a rubber mat surrounded by a pile of oxalis weed and stripping ferns from the ground. Barehanded she works in short, sharp periods before sitting back on her haunch to catch her breath.

After a few years of absence from Ballarat, Dennis is recalled to join his brothers for Noel's wedding. Noel had continued to live at Ligar Street after his father's death and has proposed to Veronica Egan. They were married at St Columba's church with Frank as best man and Dennis and the bride's brother as groomsmen ... ever a groomsman never a groom. Edna was to read the wedding details from a cutting from *The Courier* that arrived by post. Her many Ballarat friends understood the connection. After the dance, her son commenced a match with his bridesmaid. Susan was to lure him to Ballarat for many months leaving Edna to quietly resume her life with her circle of friends and neighbours. Although officially retired she accepted small jobs from her ex-boss and Bob Stewart, who owned and managed a major clothes and school uniform retailer in Kew. They had been introduced by Ray Lilford and Bob had previously used her skills.

Following the death of Joe Denman, Edna had been advised to seek compensation from his estate. Although Edna and her husband had separated they had never divorced. Consequently as his widow she sought the portion of the estate that they had jointly bought together.

Ups and Downs and Roundabouts

In the Supreme Court of Victoria: 1967.
In the matter of the Administration and Probate Act 1958 part iv as awarded Edna Irene Denman, plaintiff and Frank Thomas Denman Executor, Defendant.

A resolution in court enabled a major reduction on her loan principle and advanced the day when she could farewell the bank's monthly payments. Life now took on a more peaceful mode as the energy of the next generation passed by as her life truly became her own. She was able to find a rhythm and adjust to her son's frequent absences. Yet she was not forgotten by that generation and combined their visits with her activities and voluntary work. Quietly from retirement, another chapter began.

Eye & Ear Auxiliary

Certainly she was in demand, her doctor after her last visit asked if she could run the vacuum over his office and waiting room for a small fee. Weeks later and Ray Lilford proposed a similar arrangement. His wife had fallen and was impaired and a weekly visit would be appreciated. As each could be reached easily by bus she readily agreed. Since joining the Victorian Eye and Ear Auxiliary at the behest of her friends Betty and Jim Morgan and Margaret Collins, the Auxiliary met regularly. One venture is the sorting of paper collected from various sources and held in a local church hall. Here they bundled and packaged ton upon ton. The sale of used paper was a large income source with a ready buyer nearby with Australian Paper Mill.

Among this lively group of women, she readily fits in. Edna is quietly spoken and with hands covered in print is always busy, if not pouring tea she has a tea towel in hand. Always a doer, she would accept nothing but the odd thank you. This was her way.

15 year acknowledgement

Staying in touch

Long connected to the world by phone, total isolation was never in question. Gone are the days when we used the nearby public phone armed with a handful of pennies. Conversations between family and friends were a ready replacement for cards and letters. Yet Edna came from a generation that acknowledged events and occasions with Hallmark and other makers' cards. She enjoys the process of card selection along with the sentiment and tactile aspect, where there is space for words that can be deeply personalised.

Once more the cousins reconnected as Hilton James and his sister Kathleen joined Edna in a little light music. Beyond their reminiscences at her coffee table, they enjoyed the magic of Melbourne's musical shows. In earlier years they had patronised the Tivoli Theatre and its vaudeville shows but television had bought on its closure. Of little note was her cousins' penchant to ignore their first names and to a man and woman all used their second name. Hilton and his brother Hector never married, not so their younger sister Kath who had married an Evens. Melbourne without the Harbour Bridge had added sparkle to its resume within the arts. Dressed in her best blue suit and fox wrap, each show provided a small escape and hours of enjoyment. The Princess and Comedy Theatre seasons included *Showboat*, *There's a Girl in My Soup*, *Man of La Mancha* and *The Sound of Music*. Unlike today where Andrew Lloyd Webber's music is forefront in the audience's imagination, she had been seduced by earlier composers, like Gershwin and Lerner and Loewe and Hammerstein 11 in light opera and musical comedy.

With a little more weight and short clipped grey hair, she has become the stereotype grandmother. Alas although frequently seen with different women, her son's lifestyle is busy and elusive. She has met Julia McKay and sees the instant connection between them; maybe there is hope. He has roved to parts of the country Edna would not see. Dennis had flown to Rabaul at the invitation of John Lloyd and his wife; both were completing their internships for the Royal Melbourne Hospital. The Western Highway has been memorised to Adelaide and back as Robert Muggridge, and then Graeme and Ian had relocated through work and greener fields. He has driven the Silver City highway and crossed the Nullarbor by train.

Ebbs and flows

'Pack your bags old girl we are off to Sydney.'

Apparently hatched over a beer and forbidden to drive, Bill LePage needs to be in Sydney for his eldest son's anniversary. With a week's leave due, this mini caravan departs and follows the Princess Highway along the coast. They stop overnight at Eden before driving on to the Sydney destination.

Leaving Bill at his son's, mother and son spend the next few days' sightseeing and enjoying the lifestyle of Newport and the North Shore.

Along the length of Brougham Street, Edna is easily recognised as she goes about life. It was a time when shopping for necessities was along the strip shops of most suburban localities. At Kew, it was High Street where customers built relationships with the various shopkeepers. They knew their regulars by name and their buying patterns. Edna, like her peers, was known to the butcher, the greengrocer and many others, although supermarkets were beginning to make inroads to local shopping.

Always Something More To Do

A slower pace has replaced the quicker one of past years. There are many who share a cheery hello and others who are part of her circle. A visit to the library or to the shoe repairer can be broken with Mrs Howarth near at hand, Mrs LePage towards Malmsbury Street and Eve Hodgson or other past neighbours near number 60. With the library now located next to the new Civic Hall at Cotham Road, a simple book return is a jaunt. Kew is very different from the suburb that enclosed her from 1953. The original town hall and library in Walpole Street had closed in 1960 and was later demolished for a modern supermarket. Notably unchanged was where Cotham Road merged with High Street to leave a small promontory for the War memorial. In small pockets of this suburb she is well known for her friendship and smile.

October 1970, West Gate Bridge collapse.

Another season passes and she is advised she is to be a great aunt. Philip and Val have a daughter and she is invited to the christening. At their new home in Frankston, located at the entrance to the Mornington Peninsula, Edna is delighted to attend with son in tow. Once more Auntie Edna is fully accepted and engaged. Naturally the swish of needles and crotchet hooks has shaped the most delightful baby garments and booties. More children are born and many turn to her son as godfather. Not because of his engagement with religion but at this quiet complexity he brings to wider relationships and friendship. Edna continues to be surrounded by this wider circle.

Along with her cousins, Hilton and Kath, they still attend the odd show and share life's progress. Carol James, (granddaughter of John Alfred James) is seeking her memory of the James family as she undertakes a history of the Cornish connection. Edna's recollection of the previous generation is invaluable in opening many doors.

New phase

At the Kew branch of the Bank of New South Wales, the figure of $86.12 was the final payment on number 141 … not bad for a working mother.

Over coffee, Julia tells Edna of a trivial argument that has set them irreparably apart. Once more another young woman leaves Edna disappointed for her son. Months later and he has spoken of a random meeting between himself and a divorcee. Linda is separated with three children and they have some history from past years. They had been informally thrown together in past social settings as events and other priorities took place. They had met at Dance Court but moved in other circles.

Within the year her son has moved out and into Ashburton. Linda had recently purchased a property and together they were renovating the house. Alone for the first period of her life, the little house settles as the noise of her son's steps fade. She has spoken about the enormity of caring for stepchildren but unpersuaded he leaves with her blessing. So life takes another turn and other events draw closer.

Edna is soon introduced to this wider family and embraces a de facto nana status. Linda has two boys and a daughter. Tony aged about 10, Adrian aged eight and Louise aged five. She is welcome at Eleanor Street and can see the progress of new paint and energy that gleams all round. Once more she returns to her world of Brougham Street with her close friendships and seasonal gardening. Still, she is reminded that she is only a phone call away.

Mostly by necessity, Edna has been a busy woman all her life; but frequently it is only for the joy of giving. Not all of her evenings has been knitting for charity. She made her son's clothes as a small boy and knitted jumpers and cardigans for her brothers' children in past years, and now again for her son.

Once again her want of giving can be detailed in jumper measurements for three children.

> *Style – raglan sleeve. Tony, back 105 stiches, sleeves 53 stiches, length 31–32. Adrian, back 105, under sleeves 15, length 30–31. Louise, back 100 stiches, sleeves 51, 15 long.*

Connected and regularly visited she realises that they have to move in different paths. Once more this old girl find outlets and solace, yet her son's friends have not forgotten her and visit to show new babies and exchange stories. Occasionally she is taken to their home as she has a place in their lives. Edna continues to meet with Ettie and Eve and attend the Auxiliary monthly meeting moved from the church to the Civic Centre. It was here that she would be presented with her 15-year voluntary medal for the Eye and Ear Auxiliary. Around this period and a call of help from Ballarat brightens her day. Norm and Ada Pinney are seeking short-term accommodation for their daughter as she settles into Melbourne for teacher training. With a vacant room and the joy of helping, once more this quiet, friendly woman opens her door. Lorraine was to spend months living with Edna and forming a relationship approaching a younger daughter.

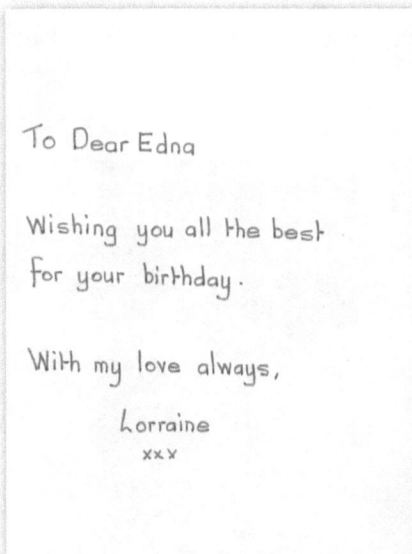

Happy birthday

A grandchild on the way

News came from Ashburton that Linda and Dennis were expecting – Edna was overjoyed. Those months passed quickly with Edna occasionally minding the children and helping as mothers do. Linda's parents lived locally in Glen Iris and were a pivotal part of recent years. Since her separation she had lived with her parents and her mother was an after school minder as Linda worked.

> **On 13 July 1976, Stuart Lloyd Denman is born.**

Edna's grandson was an early morning birth. He was born at the Cotham Road Clinic and she was told the news hours later over breakfast. If a tear was shared it was overwhelmed by the joy of my son. Stuart was born a month before her 69th birthday.

Linda and Stuart 1981

Again life settled back into the rhythm of separate lives. Her brothers were also in lock-step as their offspring moved away as business opportunities and their family circumstances changed. Philip and Val James had moved to Bathurst and memories of the full family get-togethers became distant. The celebrations of festive seasons, birthdays and births shared between the older generations moved to the next. Norm, a long time smoker, ceased overnight following a heart attack. He retired within the month. John had sold the business and moved into a small flat in Tottenham. With his children married and spread across the width of the city, he too becomes a sole resident. Other events add to Edna's enjoyment as Noel Denman has returned from years interstate with family. Her once stepson is a member of the defence forces and after stints in Sydney and Rockhampton has been deployed to Healesville. On previous holiday visits Noel has introduced his wife to Edna and she is once more a de facto nana. Steven, Anthony and Rachel are greeted warmly.

With little fuss and a few balloons, 70 years is celebrated. The wider family, including her brothers and sister-in-law, provide best wishes and share a cake. All can easily fit into the large family room at Eleanor Street. Once more grandson and grandmother share a moment before another adventure. Well-rehearsed nursery rhymes and stories always endeared toddlers and her grandson to this smiling woman. Among her favourites were 'Twinkle, twinkle little star' and 'Itsy bitsy spider'.

Precious moments shared

Her nephew Peter James and wife Ronnie, both teachers, have a small property on Coochiemudlo Island and invite her to join them. School holidays are rarely wasted in Spotswood at their home and Edna might like a change of scenery.

Ups and Downs and Roundabouts

She later related their long road trip as an adventure. Twenty plus hours with minor stops was a mighty effort on her part, tolerant and uncomplaining. The island is in the southern part of Morton Bay and accessed from Victoria Point. Coochiemudlo is a rare jewel off the Queensland coast and has remained unexploited from the time of her nephew's property purchase. The island is only accessible by ferry and its isolation is the currency of the small local number of permanent residents and day trippers. Sunsets that would remain a lifetime memory and sand the legacy of walks along the island beaches. For Edna it was possibly the only time in her 70 years that she would sample a different freedom and a tropical lifestyle. Whatever her tale it was an enriching experience and another small memento between aunt and nephew.

Her return to 141 was met with the joy of her home and its familiarity, but there was the hall of silence after constant company on the island. Once more the realisation that her life was here within her little home and time spent with family and friends precious.

Occasionally her son got it right. What a pleasure to give something in return other than her mandatory hug. The gift came unwrapped and in the form of a large colour TV. Her lounge room looked a little smaller but never to the size of modern OLED 164 cm wall units. Obviously of no comparison to the brown-eyed boy of her grandson but a small recognition of her ongoing help and support. Over the following months, visits to and visits from Eleanor Street widened as their life took on a wider circle. Edna had easily accepted her son's partner and managed to find a little common ground with the children's schooling and activities.

Surprisingly, though warm and engaging, Linda was not to be a confidante and had few, if any, women friends. Her son soon acknowledged that there were aspects of his life that was somewhat structured by past decisions, such as Linda's agreed child access to her former husband. It was right for the children but a chafe to his movement. Dennis was still working Saturday mornings although at a higher pay rate as he had progressed to a supervisor.

They were a busy family with activities in place from earlier years. The boys had joined the Hartwell scout group and attended cubs weekly. Louise attended ballet classes on Saturday mornings and Linda's parents took them to swimming lessons once a week after school. Eleanor Street continued to undergo change as the house was rejigged with inner walls removed to open space and others moved to increase family use. Once more Edna was prominent in grandchild care as the duo followed up the changes with elbow grease and paint. Outside, the effort of energy could be seen with a new bricked patio surface and consolidation of a vegetable garden. Within this plot both women could find a synergy in the joy of gardening and suitable crops for cultivation. Seen through my mother's eyes, her initial concerns may have seemed unwarranted.

Ups and Downs and Roundabouts

Parallel lives merge and enrich as life cycles continue either as a participant or an observer. Loraine Pinney has announced her engagement and soon marries to settle in East Burwood. Edna had joined Norm and Ada as the newly qualified teacher took her nuptials.

Other events continued to knock at her door as her son's friends maintain contact and visits. The Sevior's had celebrated the birth of their third child and news from Adelaide confirmed a son. Gregory Besnard was their second child to join with their daughter Andrea … Edna was much loved.

Slowing down

Links with many of her friends continued at a slower pace as her occasional bouts of shortness of breath was linked to a minor heart condition. Of similar age and also breathing heavily, her doctor prescribes the appropriate medication and advice to slow down. They agree that his waiting room cleaning can be concluded as he is considering retirement. Fortunately, there are friends able to fill her transport gaps on the occasions her son missed his cue.

Always Something More To Do

Day Tripping

Together with Ettie Barnard and the Morgans, she enjoyed Morning Melodies programs and her work for the Eye and Ear Auxiliary continued. Edna could now proudly wear her 15-year service badge presented in recognition of voluntary help. Once more change intervenes as Councils become proactive and prioritise the collection of paper and perishables. Auxiliaries and charities must turn to other forms of revenue.

Without a pause for breath Edna is whisked off to Queenscliff with Graeme and Faye Osborne, the husband and daughter of a long-time friend from her early Ballarat days. Mavis Thorpe is the last remaining link to her apprenticeship and Sturt Street. This opportune timing enables a side trip to Torquay to be reunited with her sister-in-law Tous. They have never lost contact.

Ups and Downs and Roundabouts

So the decade continued with high points of activity and longer periods of solace. Now beyond 70 years, little by little she is moved along by the aging process. They are acknowledged in our conversations, the loss of some flexibility, and shortness of breath. They are confirmed by the looking glass and the need of reading glasses and other minor afflictions. Edna was joining the queue, the first indictors of cataracts had been confirmed and another pill assisting the heart. Hands that had deftly threaded needle and kind were a little slower but still compliant to her will. Edna was still knitting children's jackets and blanket squares for the Smith family and Good Samaritan charities. Additionally she had a grandson to squander her love in kind. Stuart's measurements were listed as:

Back 82 stiches, front 82, sleeve 42 stitches, back, 9.5 inches, length 14.5 inches (1 inch = 25mm)

Ashburton hosts its first Christmas with as many of the older James and cousins as can attend. Linda's children are on holidays with their father so Edna's grandson holds centre stage. The couple are engaging and entertaining as they wine and dine this wider family. Another year is nearing completion. Dennis has now progressed to apprentice training and within the year heads the training complex. Not shared are the conversations between the couple on income and childcare. Stuart is attending childcare three mornings a week and Linda able to do a little part-time work.

More changes

Edna was later told by her son that he opted for some part-time work to help defray their income stress. Although their lifestyle was not expansive, feeding and clothing the family was consuming most of his income. The impact soon became apparent, as her son began working most weekends and his visits to Brougham Street less frequent. Linda periodically filled the gap to keep grandson and grandmother in touch. Her son regardless of his weekend workloads still manages a grocery run and small jobs outside her reach.

Times changed and friends went missing or moved into care or passed on. Edna's surviving brothers were not forgotten by age and health issues during this period. Norm and Gwen had moved out of the family home and relocated to a unit in Ringwood. Once more health issues became the catalyst of decisions. John, after sole trading, had worked for the defence department till pension age. Since retirement he has been captured by his children's decision; he could no longer live alone. He packed his bags and relocated to his daughter and son-in-law's home near Gisborne.

Birthdays celebrated, christenings and events passed in sequence and the wider family is separated by distance and age. The ripple of the younger generations continues to spread as another decade approaches. Stuart is now at primary school and Adrian and Louise progress through high school. Linda's eldest Tony has completed his VCE and opted to do chemical engineering at Warrnambool TAFE. Change is ever present. Yet there is still another page to be turned for this old girl. Bev and Chas Cornell after years of moving between statewide locations have bought a large block in Mathoura and suggest a visit.

Edna has known the couple from before their wedding and between Eve Hodgson and letters has kept in touch. Bev confirms that when next in town Edna should have her bag ready. Whatever the quality or underscored warmth this old girl is a magnet to people. Born in Western Australia, Chas Cornell is at heart a bushman and after Korea, worked as a builder before navigating the state in the police force. Bev has followed this roving life and finally has a settled home for her children … another family for Edna's embrace. She has seen Bev's children's progress in snapshots and attended the eldest daughter's wedding. She can now receive a hug and share a story. Her time there was engaging and relaxing as she is approaching her 77th year. A number of photos of her, yellow bucket in hand feeding the kangaroo and chooks are insightful and a delight to the eye. Slowing down she might be, but the will is still strong.

Life with Bev and Chas Cornell

Separation

On what should have been a quiet Sunday afternoon exchange her son related that their romance is over and he and Linda have agreed to separate. His concern for his son is paramount but feels that he is better left in his family unit. Reasons of why or how are always complex and would remain best unsaid as both sides move on. Both understood the breakup would scar this small boy like others before ... her son had trod that path. Dennis would take a week's leave and find a flat and reorganise the next period of his life. If Edna shed more tears after his departure she never shared this moment with her son but remained solid in support. He moves to Camberwell, mid-point between Eleanor Street and Brougham Street and this was to be his nest for some years. She was to provide not only moral support but many items of kitchen and bedroom necessities. Regrettably others had made difficult life decisions earlier that year and divorce is confirmed for Barry James. Added to the list is Lorraine Pinney as she too parted company. She was to move close by in Kew and visit regularly. Edna was an ear and shoulder for more than her son.

Edna understood that there would be no winners from this family breakdown and that her grandson would be confused and hurt. She was to provide a loving environment with every visit. The following year consolidated access as she shared the investment in her grandson. Sundays were set aside as she provided a second home experience for 'her two boys'. Here she could provide her grandson with small comforts as their relationship grew. She took him on walks and to the park as well as playing games and helping with his ABCs. The Sunday roast for so much a staple of her life was replaced as the trio found the Pizza Hut and its selections. This was to be the pattern for the coming years as they progressed to wider entertainment and began to enjoy each other's company. Stuart's drawings of shapes and symbols including letters from the alphabet became part of her keepsakes.

A milestone birthday

Eighty years old and another milestone to celebrate as she sees her eighth decade. Her door will remain open as her family and friends arrive during the week and over the weekend. Her demeanour remains steadfast and straight of carriage. Her hair is now the colour of snow and her skin remains unblemished. The cataract operation has been successful but she notices that her right eye has diminished sight. The eye specialist confirms her sight has diminished to be legally blind. Her love of reading which she has shared with her son is easier with large print. She remains inclusive and warm and has time for all. Flowers and presents in keeping with her mantra of no fuss line her mantelpiece and card table. Fortunately her visitors don't all come as one as space and chairs are somewhat limited.

Boroondara aged-care services

Ups and Downs and Roundabouts

Strangely, the failure of his marriage has consolidated her son's ambition as he divides his life with a new energy. Acknowledging that Stuart's progress is mainly in his mother's keeping, he embraces his role in support and companionship. Her son has become fiercely independent and income is his first priority. Promotion at work has progressed to a corporate position and he continues nightly and weekends market research where possible. Brougham Street has benefited from this energy and a replacement front fence completed as well as the house exterior being painted. As the word spreads of his changed circumstances close friends unite and draw closer. Another constant has been the friendship these many years of Ray and Joan Sevior who made their home hers for many functions and always a seat at their table. The Sevior's hospitality returns as though a decade was misplaced and kindness is showered on Edna and her son. They join the other Mrs D (Joan's mum) and Ray's father at many festive periods. The Sevior's are more than dear friends.

With Stuart at high school he is slowly withdrawing to a group of friends and is gradually drawn away from Brougham street visits. He has joined her son at the Olinda Golf Club and is a talented junior. Edna's disappointment is apparent, but she understands the gap between generations. A bout of influenza slows her down but never from the point of unbalancing her life. This decade is to test her qualities as 'father time' looks on. She has taken a 'few turns' in her words and the doctor has upped her medication. Once more she acknowledges that her family and remaining friends bring her the most joy. She has become a spectator and witness to events of loved ones and friends. Dennis has purchased his own unit in Hawthorn and is close by for emergencies. Lorraine Pinney is a constant and will remarry to live near at hand. Jim and Betty call frequently and drive her about. The roll call of lost ones is ever increasing and casts a shadow on her days. Still others have left or passed away and she occasionally mentions many of her friends are gone.

Stuart has spent the afternoon embellishing his final years of high school and shares a picture of his Year 12 formal, resplendent in his tux and bow tie. Within the year he will commence a career working for OPSM. Edna is witness to another achievement as she watches her son accepting his Graduate Diploma from Swinburne University of Technology in December of 1993.

Events have merged the years as brother John and sister are reunited to compare notes and enjoy their families' growth with Barry James and Maria, his second wife, and daughter hosting a family get-together.

Daily life continued with a degree of uniformity. Edna had opted for aspects of the Boroondara aged services with meals on wheels and fortnightly cleaning. She supplements the meals with fresh vegetables and other condiments as she had no wish to walk away from her kitchen. Here within this space were the memories of meals and preparation.

Ups and Downs and Roundabouts

The pleasure of guests that shared a homemade scone or biscuits at her table was a joy. Her son's relish of her egg and bacon pie and brick sized pasties bought her pleasure but much time in preparation.

Mum was an exceptional home cook, yet there was a rare occasion where a dish had gone wanting. Vegetable soup under low simmer was nearing competition and sampled for taste. A little more pepper would see it right and so ... the lid came off the pepper pot and half the contents added.

Edna scooped and boiled the soup to recover but at the table mother and son through tears of heat and laughter finally passed.

The benefit of the aged service was eyes on and a friendly face at the door. Weekends could see any number of distractions as the Pinneys dropped in between visiting their adult children or other friends. Sundays were a little different without her grandson in sight. Stuart had recently moved away from home and joined a few mates in renting a house in Mount Waverley. Family contact was maintained between brother and sister with Gloria, her husband, Stan and children able to bring John and Edna together. Likewise, her son could ferry her to Sunbury and Ringwood as required. Norm's health had also declined in these latter years and he requires a ride-on to help with the local shopping. In concert was an oxygen kit to assist breathing spells as required, a warning to all ex-smokers.

Family ties and goodbyes

Keeping Edna in touch with her family became a priority of her son and many an afternoon was spent over coffee and biscuits. It was additionally a time when the Sunday drive was her window into the city's world. New and old suburbs had been renewed and changed the face of Melbourne. High-rise buildings and towers filled her eye as every other week we navigated the city and outer suburbs. So much change to take in and discuss when a normal day was limited to 50 metres from her gate. This was her exercise regime with a far fence to sit on if required. Though still bright in herself, the colours of age were apparent. Her face was a little drawn and the odd liver spot sat on the back of her hands, all references for her son if he was to ever match her years. Yet never a complaint was uttered and each day another challenge. Far from her gate, politics have never been a major part of Edna's lifestyle: like all in the community we vote at elections and receive little or nothing for our efforts. Not so her son, who over many years had held positions in labour unions and professional associations. That was not really a consideration as he explained that with major transport reforms and restructures his qualifications should be updated. In the following year he commenced a Diploma of Education. Two years on and Edna was to celebrate another of life's milestones as her son turned 50.

These years had hurried on and a 'turn' sees these older family members hospitalised. Norm was in the Heidelberg

Repatriation hospital returned service section and Edna rushed by ambulance to the Austin Hospital emergency ward. It was her heart that triggered this episode and she will return again in future months as again it conspires to slow her down. Within the year Norm had succumbed to his heart condition and the second of her brothers died, aged 84. Norm was survived by his wife Gwen, two adult children and seven grandchildren. He was in the main a quiet man and genuinely loved by his sons and grandchildren. Their sobs and words of remembrance at his funeral were a fitting tribute to their grandfather. My happiest recollection was of an unassuming compassionate man and the laughter he exhibited when he trumped or took a trick in the family's competitive card games.

Norm's 80th Birthday

CHAPTER 8

Journey's End

All night long I sat in a long corridor with my mother. During this period I intermittingly held tight to her hand as we briefly exchanged the odd utterances. Mum was very clammy and her breathing varied but was mostly shallow. Why she remained on that gurney during this period has never been clarified but I suspect either a bed shortage or an implication of departure. On occasion an attendant or nurse passed by with a 'she's breathing' comment and in the early morning I confronted a doctor for an assessment.

His response confirmed his reservations on her surviving the night – now she would slowly recover with care. A testament to her courage.

On reflection, this was not the first in her journey as we had trod this path before. Many months earlier on returning from an afternoon drive, Mum collapsed at the gate. Lifting her from the footpath and into the house and bed was a struggle. In my heart, it was goodbye, and I silently said farewell. It was not to be – within half an hour, a GP had assessed her condition and the first of her ambulance rides occurred. Released and in brighter spirits with an 'on watch' review and a change in medication we returned her to 141. I stayed a couple of days to a level of comfort and became ever more watchful and visible. It was during this period that we talked and I taped her childhood recollections and memories of those early days. We spoke about periods of her childhood and she added forgotten moments when we talked about her brother George.

'George only worked at Crocker's. He started work from school at 14 and a half as a messenger boy on a bike and then into haberdashery. From there he went into manchester, selling sheets and the like before the dress and curtain material counter. He wrote all the tickets, dressed mannequins and when they had a sale dressed the window displays. With all that knowledge, he then went travelling before being second in command in the men's department. They paid for his medical expenses to Melbourne and then his funeral expenses. You were only 12 months old when he died.'

Consequently she rallied and returned to home with support services and doctors' visits. Fortunately I had flexibility in my work role and could visit for an hour or two depending on her needs. Those friends in the loop were additionally able to support us both as I made arrangements for education deferral and finalised all legal documentation. It was a provoking period as the future and her hopes slowly ebbed away. Mum confronted this period with the realisation she may not be able to continue in her home.

Her next 'turn' saw her once more carried to the Austin & Repatriation Medical Centre and admitted to the cardiac ward. Her stay there drifted beyond days and soon beyond a month. I was able to visit almost every day, either late afternoon or evenings as my flexible arrangements with work dictated. While she was in the best of care her mood and thoughts were always about her return to home. During her stay others brightened her mood, her sister-in-law Gwen, Lorraine Hunt and finally her grandson appeared. To rationalise how this visit and hug could so lift her spirits is difficult to express, but it returned a ray of hope.

Regrettably her health issues had again conspired against her and the assessment team pronounced 'hostel care'. The pin was pulled in February 1996 after consultation with the manager of Social Services and the decision taken from our hands. Mum was to commence her next journey, to Parkland Close. Parkland was located in Childers Road and was within walkable distance from Brougham Street. It was important not to dislocate her from her home suburb and the remaining friends who would visit. Her acceptance of this new situation was another act of selflessness, as in her eyes a necessity. In essence she decided that I couldn't or shouldn't look after her. At the time it was considered a short-term stay but without an alternative it was a possible home. I had walked the pavements and during this period looked at other aged care residences from Kew to Heidelberg, but this property met my care criteria. Vacancies and time become a premium. Within days we had relocated her necessities and those special items that would reaffirm by sight and touch Brougham Street. Mum was able to assemble her clothes of choice and other items that were of personal significance. Closing the door, I realised this was in some ways an ending but she held on to the thought of HOPE.

Hamer Court

Mum's time at Childers Road was comfortable and with full-time care she seemed to rally. Well enough to receive other visitors and able to enjoy a Sunday drive and briefly visit 141. During this period she indicated that should a vacancy arrive at Hamer Court she would be happy to relocate. How her knowledge of Hamer Court or its desirability came about remains unknown, yet the net was cast and months later a vacancy occurred. The proximity of these two locations is a matter of half a block so it was a relatively easy task for me to move Mum without additional help. If a snail can carry its home on its back then the message was clear to both my mother and me. Two or three trips with the car made it all possible. A choice of rooms enabled 'a room with a view' overlooking a garden, with filtered light to engage with.

With a little uncertainty, Mum settled into her new bed-sit with the realisation that this might signify a final separation from her little home. We discussed the improbability of her return and that her health issues had become the main concern. Her discharge assessment from the Austin, although positive in most self-care indicators confirmed help in areas of mobility and showering. With another big breath and unsteady step she began her next journey. The facility was highly regarded and carried the name of a former premier. Besides its inside décor, it had an outside area and garden, a library, a social room and a population of wonderful carers.

She was quickly acknowledged as a non-complaining wonder. Hamer Court and staff enabled a pause in my own life and an opportunity to set about the 'to do' list. Beyond her deposit the deferred down payment needed to be part of a financial assessment ... rent or sell.

Always Something More To Do

Edna with Steven & David Katula 1990 (Grand nephews)

Her new life was to become a little regimented as the system of care commenced to provide health and personal services as well as activities. Not so her social period as a steady stream of family and friends came to her door. Those local friends and acquaintances know how valued their kindness, but some should be acknowledged. Graeme and Raelene Besnard and daughter combined a visit to his parents and always made time for my mother. There was nothing new in their regular visits to her home since becoming residents of Virginia (SA). To my mother they were family by default. Her joy was palpable in sharing her surrounds and the high tea provided. Andrea was caught between moods of joy and sadness as she was to return to her life in Japan.

Journey's End

Weeks turned to months and our routine of occasional drives and house visits became the norm, another jacket, another skirt and a few personal items ... decisions deferred, now made. Her home was to be sold. Brougham Street was auctioned in April 1997. Edna Irene Denman sat quietly in my car opposite her home as the bid was finalised. What's done is done.

Her last period at Hamer Court was of comfort and a degree of happiness. She realised that she was not or never would be forgotten and once more her friends and family filled many hours. John and Mum exchanged their memories and the progress of this next generation. Unfortunately this period had seen late night medical interventions and a return to Austin Hospital. She has now entered her 89th year and is determined to see her grandson's coming of age, aka 21. Edna treasured his birthday card and Stuart's words once more filled her with joy...

Dear Nan,
Well it's been a battle but you've pulled and fought through again.
All my best for your 89th birthday and warmest regards for the future.
Lots of love,
your grandson,
Stuart

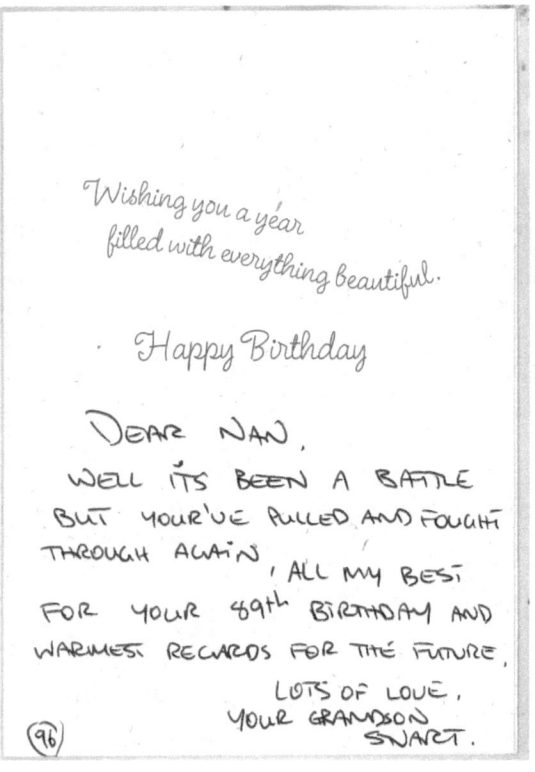 

Happy birthday Nan

This final period at Hamer Court was marked with apprehension as her body battled against its tormentors. The nurses and staff were close at hand and her near and dear ever close. Yet journeys are not always shared and time and disease continued to take their toll. Moments of shared hours together continued and long walks were now on hold. A walk around the patio was slow and measured but courageous and dignified. Where all meals had previously been part of the common community most were now taken in her room.

Journey's End

The winter of this year had once more confirmed her fragility when hospitalisation for brief periods occurred. The last episode saw her reinstated at the Austin Medical Centre and now assessed as requiring nursing home care. The nicest of social workers took me through the decision, but the words were stark on the pages. The transfer to a vacancy in any of the abovementioned nursing homes will occur. The care plan was dated 18 July 1997. Mum had fulfilled a silent wish to hear that five days earlier her grandson had attained 21. Later that day I sat with Mum and relayed the news. She was a little confused but stressed that she would be okay in a day or to. I could only hold her hand and agree.

Any moistening of the eye is but a minor distraction. Phone calls and visits were shrouded in the fog of aged care needs and approaching grief. This time there was to be only a brief rally. Her condition rapidly slid and within a week, Mum was relocated to Caritas Christi, Kew. Daily visits were confronting and on the day I faced the inevitable she passed away. I had sat with her this morning without her recognition, her breath shallow as nursing staff told me she was comfortable. Vale Mum.

She concluded her journey a few days after her 90th birthday with little celebration other than a gentle embrace. To her many friends who enriched her life I am truly thankful. To those who she touched and shared moments with, there are memories.

Edna Irene may well have prized these words.

Make new friends but keep the old; one is silver and the other gold.

About the Author

On the 25th anniversary of her passing, her son attempted to put together the journey of her life in hope that her great grandchildren will gain an insight into the times and challenges of an early 20th century woman's life.

The stories told have been shared from the memory of past events and in Dennis's own words from Edna's conversations in the later part of her life.

www.ingramcontent.com/pod-product-compliance
Lightning Source LLC
Chambersburg PA
CBHW021150080526
44588CB00008B/284